# 39 MICROLECTURES

## in proximity of performance

A series of accidents has brought you to this book.

You may think of it not as a book, but as a library, an elevator, an amateur performance in a nearby theatre.

Open it to the table of contents.

Turn it to the page that sounds the most interesting to you.

Read a sentence or two.

Repeat the process.

Read this book as a creative act, and feel encouraged.

*39 Microlectures: in proximity of performance* is a collection of miniature stories, parables, musings and thinkpieces on the nature of reading, writing, art, collaboration, performance, life, death, the universe and everything. It is a unique and moving document for our times, full of curiosity and wonder, thoughtfulness and pain.

Matthew Goulish, the founder member of performance group Goat Island, meditates on these and other diverse themes, proving, along the way, that the boundaries between poetry and criticism, and between creativity and theory, are less fixed than they seem. The book is revelatory, solemn yet at times hilarious, and written to inspire – or perhaps provoke – creativity and thought.

**Matthew Goulish**, performer and writer, has collaborated on the creation of seven performance works with the group Goat Island. He teaches at the School of the Art Institute of Chicago.

First published 2000 by Routledge
11 New Fetter Lane, London EC4P 4EE

Simultaneously published in the USA and Canada
by Routledge
29 West 35th Street, New York, NY 10001

Reprinted 2001

*Routledge is an imprint of the Taylor & Francis Group*

Typeset in Joanna and Scala by Florence Production Ltd, Stoodleigh, Devon

Printed and bound in Great Britain by
TJ International Ltd, Padstow, Cornwall

*British Library Cataloguing in Publication Data*
A catalogue record for this book is available from the British Library

*Library of Congress Cataloging in Publication Data*
Goulish, Matthew, 1960–
    39 microlectures : in proximity of performance / Matthew Goulish.
        p.   cm.
    Includes bibliographical references.
I. Title: Thirty-nine microlectures.   II. Title.
PS3557.09135 A615 2000
818'.607–dc21                                                    00-020374

ISBN 0-415-21393-2 (pbk)
ISBN 0-415-21392-4 (hbk)

Microlectures 0–2.3, 4.1–4.3, 7.1–7.5, 9.1–9.5, 11.1   *for my parents*

Microlectures 3.1–3.3, 8.1–8.3   *for my students*

Microlectures 10.1–10.3   *for those departed*

Introduction 1, Microlecture 00   *for whom it may concern*

Introduction 2–5, Microlectures 5.1–5.3   *for Lin*

# CONTENTS

## ACKNOWLEDGMENTS

Cavafy, C. P., *Waiting for the Barbarians*. Copyright © 1992 by Edmund Keeley and Philip Sherrard. Reprinted by permission of Princeton University Press.

Dennis Cooper, lines from the poem "Drugs" reprinted from *The Tenderness of the Wolves*. Copyright © 1982 The Crossing Press. Reprinted by permission of the author.

Russell Edson, selections from "The Ceremony" and "A Man with a Tree on His Head" are reprinted from *The Tunnel*. Copyright © 1994 Oberlin College Press. Reprinted by permission of Oberlin College Press.

Lines from *The Little Mariner*, copyright © 1988 by Odysseas Elytis, translated by Olga Broumas. Reprinted by permission of Copper Canyon Press, Post Office Box 271, Port Townsend, WA 98368.

Lines by Susan Howe, from *Pierce-Arrow*, copyright © 1999 Susan Howe. Reprinted by permission of New Directions Publishing Corp.

Lines from Verses 16, 92, 93, 95, 97, and 101 of *Gitanjali* by Rabindranath Tagore. Reprinted by permission of Branden Publishing Company.

Lines from *My Life* by Lyn Hejinian reprinted by permission of Sun & Moon Press.

Every attempt has been made to secure permission for copyright material. If any copyright holder has been inadvertently omitted, please apply in writing to the publisher.

## 1. TO THE READER-1

When reading this book, please take your time. Remember that you do not necessarily need to start at the beginning. Start anywhere; stop anywhere. Don't worry about reaching the end. Don't read the whole book if you don't want to. Look through the table of contents, and start at the point that sounds most interesting to you. Read one line repeatedly for two days. Do whatever you need to with this book, and, if possible, do not let it damage your thoughts. Put it down, and read something else. Read this book as a creative act.

Of course, reading is always a creative act, and you may read any book this way. But in this case, feel encouraged.

I did not intend this book to have a beginning, an end, or a middle. I did not intend it to become a book at all. I intended to pull together thoughts that I considered important. I wanted to express them by letting them sit next to one another. Now those thoughts have become a book, and acquired certain undeniable qualities of bookness, including beginnings, ends, and middles. One may enjoy these as such and feel thankful for tradition.

However, this book also represents a meeting place of many books, a catalogue, and can we consider that a book? Early writers used beech bark paper, or even inscribed on trees. Today we print on recycled paper, not so much on what was once a tree as on what was more recently another book. Consider this book recycled – less a book, and more a micro-library, and as a library resembles memory, this book exists in the past. You read a sentence that you may have read before. You may conclude that we live in an accelerated time. Sometimes time itself seems to threaten to disappear. Maybe we need new thoughts less than we need to decelerate, to reduce our thoughts, to refold them into other thoughts, and to recycle them.

With that in mind, you may want to avoid reading this book altogether. Go directly to the source notes, and read the books from which I have quoted and misquoted.

Writers with far more experience than myself wrote them. Why then does this book exist?

Consider this book like an interrupted performance. The writer left the stage because of a sudden illness, which has now become prolonged. The writer will not return. I have been asked to stand in. Thank you for this distinction and this honor. I will do my best to complete the performance, to patch it together, and fulfill the writer's intentions. Please remember I am only a substitute. In order to fulfill those intentions, I will not imitate them, but only point to them. I will need your help. You must read creatively. Please take your time. Remember that you do not necessarily need to start at the beginning. Start anywhere; stop anywhere. Don't worry about reaching the end. Don't read the whole book if you don't want to. Look through the table of contents, and start at the point that sounds most interesting to you. Read one line repeatedly for two days. Do whatever you need to with this book, and, if possible, do not let it damage your thoughts. Put it down, and read something else. Read this book as a creative act. Always remember that this book is not important. That other writer, that other performance, that other book that will now never be written — that was the necessary one.

## 2. WHAT IS A BOOK?

### 2.1 The open book

Existence is not infinity, but that which allows the existant to be thought of as deriving from infinity.

For example, I was once nineteen years old and kneeling on the floor in a library in Kalamazoo, Michigan. There, below the bottom shelf of the theatre section, I found a cardboard box containing back issues of the *Tulane Drama Review*. I read about Bertolt Brecht, Julian Beck and Judith Malina, Joseph Chaikin, Happenings. I read fragments — a line, a paragraph, a page — like that, on my knees, then I replaced the journal into the box, slightly embarrassed by this activity. Growing up in the midwest in the 1960s and 1970s meant never seeing performances like this. If I could not see the performances, I could at least look at the pictures. I studied the photographs of Richard Foreman's Ontological-Hysteric Theatre: unbalanced posed tableaux, contorted performers wearing hybrid costumes in exaggerated rooms, lengths of white cord stretched through the air. This is something new, I thought. The film society screened Werner Herzog's *Every Man for Himself and God Against All, The Mystery of Kaspar Hauser*. Kaspar has been stabbed. With blood spreading on the front of his shirt, he walks quickly through a garden, his upper body stiff and leaning back, a young boy leading him by the hand. Maybe, I thought, this is how the people move across the stage in The Ontological-Hysteric Theatre of Richard Foreman.

I received a book from my theatre professors as a gift: *Lunatics, Lovers and Poets, the contemporary experimental theatre* by Margaret Croyden. My distracting embarrassment, one might say, moved to center stage. I read and re-read the book, especially the passage on page 170, describing a group called The Open Theatre.

During the early and mid-1960's, every morning a group of young people could be seen hurrying into a dilapidated old building on West Fourteenth Street. A creaky broken-down elevator took them to a messy loft five flights above the dirt and noise of the street. Upstairs it was quiet, relaxed, friendly. The group would be sipping their morning coffee. Then they would go onto mats and start their sound and body exercises. Everyone would slowly wake up.

What attracted me to this passage? It must have been the sense of community, of creative work, of waking up, and most of all, of the creaky broken-down elevator.

Consider the performance of the elevator. The role the elevator plays in buildings and its revolutionary potential make it a very dangerous instrument. It completely undermines, annihilates, and ridicules architectural abilities. It ridicules compositional instincts, annihilates education, and undermines the doctrine that there must always be an architectural means to shape transitions. The great achievement of the elevator is its ability to establish connections within a building without any recourse to architecture. Where architecture, in order to make connections, has to go through incredibly complicated gestures, the elevator simply ridicules, bypassing all knowledge, and establishing connections mechanically.

I found a record: Béla Bartók's *Concerto for Orchestra*, played by the Israel Philharmonic, conducted by Zubin Mehta, in a brown record jacket with a reproduction of a painting by Paul Klee called *The Open Book*. The book, seen from above, unfolded its pages in all directions – left to right, top to bottom, impossible triangulations near the center. It looked like an oversized flower, a brown rectilinear artichoke opening. No, it looked like a miniature model for a city. It doesn't matter what it looked like. Why describe it? It was a painting of a book unfolding on the jacket of a vinyl recording of music in Kalamazoo in 1979. In Elegia, the third movement, (band 3, side 1), the strings play a three-note theme, over a dissonant orchestral soundbed, conjuring feelings of inconceivable destruction and sadness, as if to say, "What man has inflicted on man, in very recent times – the sum and potential of human behavior – presses on the brain with a new kind of darkness. An open book is also night."

A simple question occurred to me then. Can this be what people mean when they talk about beauty? Eventually I walked into the Peggy Guggenheim Museum in Venice and found Paul Klee's painting, *The Open Book*. Immediately I heard the remorseful three note theme of the Elegia, the third movement, (band 3, side 1), of Bartok's Concerto for Orchestra. Since the first time I heard it, twenty years had passed.

## 2.2 Where there is wind

In 1998, the newspaper *India Today* reported the following.

By afternoon the wind had fallen silent over Pokhran. At 3:45 P.M., the timer detonated the three devices. 300 m deep in the earth, the heat generated was equivalent to a million degrees centigrade – as hot as temperatures on the sun. Instantly, rocks weighing a thousand tonnes, a mini mountain underground, vapourised . . . shockwaves from the blasts began to lift a mound of earth the size of a football field. One scientist on seeing it said, 'I can now believe stories of Lord Krishna lifting a hill.'

After witnessing the first successful atom bomb test in New Mexico in 1945 J. Robert Oppenheimer quoted from the same source.

I remembered the line from the Hindu scripture, the Bhagavad-Gita. Vishnu is trying to persuade the prince that he should do his duty, and to impress him takes on his multi-armed form and says, 'Now I am become death, the destroyer of worlds.' We knew that the world would not be the same.

The difference of the world, in the twentieth century's second half, has been, like Krishna's many forms, a series of repetitions. The blast in the New Mexico desert marked the beginning of this endlessness. Its first practical application, at 8:15 on the morning of August 6, 1945, killed 300,000 people. It also killed the idea of the executioner. A crew member of the Enola Gay was able to say a few hours after dropping the bomb over Hiroshima, "I knew the Japs were in for it, but I felt no particular emotion about it."

Now we require nothing productive of our victims, but only the mathematical performance of their death – an instantaneous transformation from human being to useless residue – for audiences around the world.

We have manufactured death with such perfection that life feels counterfeit. The result that the exact moment when the act of atrocity begins now eludes us, as does its end, or its limit. The sum and potential of human behavior presses on the imagination with a new kind of darkness. Like science and politics, our words have betrayed us: our languages, our silences, complicit in our violent and complex poverty. Now we think of knowledge as that from which we must escape in order to create, to find a place to call a beginning, and another place to call an end. No matter how responsible, irresponsible, how personal, wise, or innocent, how clear or unintelligible our creations, we feel they commune in devalued currencies, in criminally suspect vocabularies. No matter how much we write, we are left with the feeling there is more to say.

Consider the book that will now never be written, full of uselessness and accidents, the book which places our distractions and our embarrassments center stage, unfolds them like an artichoke, allows us to escape ourselves, impedes our terrible progress. Consider the necessary book of elevators, and music from twenty years ago, the book of strange invitations, about which we can say, "This book is not a book. It's not a song. Nor a poem. Nor thoughts." On the verge of irreconcilability, I turned over a rock, and made a discovery. Can this be what people mean when they talk about beauty? I considered a book that might result from following some simple instructions: 1) fill your book with seeds, 2) cut holes in it, 3) hang it where there is wind.

## 3. WHAT IS A FACT?

### 3.1 Thanksgiving-1: The impossible is a frog

We began on Thanksgiving Day, 1986 – Lin Hixson, the brothers Timothy McCain and Greg McCain, and I. Eventually others joined us – Karen Christopher, Bryan Saner, Mark Jeffery. But on that first day in 1986, when the four of us met in my apartment on W. Caton Street, Wicker Park, Chicago, we did not know we were beginning a performance group or even that we were beginning a performance. We only knew that we were beginning. We agreed that we would share a kind of impossible problem from which we would generate material individually, and then come together: a starting point.

> Choose a specific incident from your past. Find
> a historical event that occurred at approximately
> the same time.
>
> Create an environment and/or performance
> expressing the feeling of the memory in relation
> to the historical incident.

We had no idea where this would lead us, or when it would lead us there. We simply agreed to begin, and then went out for Thanksgiving dinner. At the suggestion of a friend we eventually named our performance group Goat Island.

We had few skills and little understanding of performance. We unanimously elected Lin Hixson director. We needed confidence, and for that we turned to Lin. She introduced us to the work of Pina Bausch from Germany, and Butoh dance from Japan. She showed us a paragraph by Yvonne Rainer from 1965.

> NO to spectacle no to virtuosity no to
> transformations and magic and make believe no to
> the glamour and transcendency of the star image

no to the heroic no to the anti-heroic no to trash
imagery no to involvement of performer or
spectator no to style no to camp no to seduction
of spectator by the wiles of the performer no to
eccentricity no to moving or being moved.

We admired these words. They encouraged us to avoid almost everything. What remained worth attempting, of course, seemed equally impossible. What could we do but emulate others who had attempted the impossible before us? In 1987, we invited Tatsumi Hijikata, legendary Japanese dancer and founder of Butoh, to join our company. His death in 1986 made him available. He accepted, and he often visited our rehearsals in the form of a ghost, taking part in discussions, delicately responding to our starting point.

Hijikata:
*Now I am a frog far away from the shadow of an idea.*

Over the years we began to work many times, directionless except for our starting point.

Describe the last time you had sex.
Create an event of bliss/create an event of terror.
Why were you in pain in such a beautiful place?
Create a shivering homage.
Invent an arrival.
How do you say goodbye?

Lin Hixson:
*I look for phrases that can be performed as a task. Viewing movement as a piece of work or as a difficult or tedious undertaking gives us, who have little formal training in dance, a way into the physical; a way to draw from the everyday; the familiar and the mundane.*

I feel thankful now for this collection of beginnings. Each one allowed us a kind of simplicity, as though each movement, or cell of movement, were a physical fact. We could align the physical facts with the facts of words, ideas, or music – the simplicity of fact: their selection, expression, and arrangement. There are oceans of facts.

*Example #1: devouring*

Hijikata:

Early spring was the busy season on the farm. Everyone went out to work in the fields. There was no one in the neighboring houses. Children three or four years old were tied to large pillars in every home. I would sneak over to take a peek at those little kids. They made strange movements; one fed food to his own hand — what an odd thing to do! Of course he was not old enough to be conscious of his self. At any rate, I was engrossed in watching this when the child's mother returned, and said, 'What is it? You like kids? Please, don't come back tomorrow!' This made me feel somewhat uneasy. It was all because I went back to peek at them too often. The child was treating his hand as if it weren't a part of himself. It was as if it wasn't his own hand. He probably felt that he was someone else.

Karen lost a great deal of weight suddenly. She found out she had diabetes. We continued working on the performance, with Karen in the role of Mike Walker, America's fattest man, at 1,187 pounds, a veteran of the Korean war, and a sideshow performer. We transcribed his recorded speech, and Karen performed it.

Mike Walker:

I was like you once. In Korea, I weighed two hundred pounds. Then, in medical terms, I suffered a severe psychological effect which brought latent neuroses to the surface, mine being strong suicidal tendencies manifesting themselves in a compulsive eating symptom. In plain, everyday language this means I gave up, and tried to destroy myself by gorging myself with food. I ate constantly, getting larger and larger, until I reached the unreal weight of one thousand one hundred and eighty-seven pounds. I am unable to walk. The doctors have given me only a few months to live. I now see how I have wrecked my life, and also affected the lives of ones dear to me, my wife and my son and my mother. I have decided to place myself on exhibit in an effort to discourage the public, especially teenagers, from wrecking their lives the way I have wrecked mine. If I can stop one person, then my life has some meaning. On the other side of this record you can hear my song, telling you more about my problems and my physical condition.

One might find elements of autobiography inverted in the biography of another — the trope of a factual life, performed by a stand-in.

Hijikata:

Taking into your own body the idea that your wrist is not your own — there's an important secret hidden in this concept. The basis of dance is concealed there.

The question is: Do they mean it when they say No Trespassing?

## Example #2: collapsing

We see ourselves as process immersed in process beyond ourselves. We break the rules, even our own rules. And how do we do that? By leaving plenty of room for X quantities.

Timothy McCain:
*When we first work on a piece, Lin asks us to bring in what interests us at the time. We don't know where it's going to go or what's going to happen. You bring in that your foot was run over by a car. Or whatever. You present that to the group.*

This grasp of factuality is one extreme of thought. Namely, it is the concept of mere agitation of things agitated. Tim repeatedly watched the television footage of then-President George Bush getting sick in Japan. He interpreted the President's movements as dance.

Timothy McCain:
*Butoh Bush is done in the seated position. The top half of the body leans back but the shoulders are off the floor. The legs raise off the floor about six inches. The arms float over the chest and stomach. When George Bush was in Japan, he became ill and vomited. The Secret Service man held Bush off the floor and the cameras showed him in a position that seemed very Butoh.*

Process is the immanence of the infinite in the finite. There is no reason to hold that confusion is less fundamental than is order.

## interruption: first words, not last words

As will quickly become apparent to the reader, this book is an exploration, a first word, not a last word, an attempt to capture ideas. The convention of sincerity discourages me. I write because of the good fortune I have to get mixed up in everything.

## Example #3: haunting

I found a photograph of a kabuki actor in the book *Childhood Years* by Jun'ichiro Tanizaki. It had this accompanying description.

I may not have fully appreciated Kyuzo's artistry, but I was thrilled by his portrayal of Tomomori dressed as a ghost, wearing white-laced armor with arrows embedded in it; and by the part where Tomomori winds an anchor rope around his body and throws himself backward from a rock into the sea. I was so impressed by it that later I often played at 'Tomomori with the anchor,' wearing an improvised suit of cardboard armor in the Kairakuen storeroom or in the parlor at Yukiuchi the wigmaker's house.

I carried a copy of the photograph around for several months without showing it to anyone. It did not seem to fit with our starting point at the time. (Create a shivering homage. Create a trembling homage.) Then we invited Bryan Saner to join the company. He accepted.

Matthew:
*Do you think Bryan sometimes looks like a ghost?*

Lin:
*Yes, he can be very otherworldly.*

I introduced the kabuki photo into rehearsals. Bryan took it with him to a family reunion in South Dakota. He returned with an old, rusted iron plow.

Bryan Saner:
*Last Christmas I went back to visit our home farm. My Uncle gave me some parts of our old plow with which to build an anchor for the Goat Island show. The sun was just setting, and I remembered how as a child I would be so sad to see the day end that I would cry for no other reason.*

Hijikata:
*We should take good care of our deceased. We've got to bring our dead close to us and lead our lives with them. The dead are my teachers.*

No fact is merely itself. The earth rotates, and we move with it.

## 3.3 The meeting place

Srinivasa Ramanujan was born in southern India in 1887. His development of the mathematics of elliptical integrals, partitions, analytic number theory, and infinite-series expansions of trigonometric and circular functions, earned him the distinction of the first Indian elected Fellow of the Royal Society in England. He died at age 33. His final notebooks have contributed to the recent revolutionary concept in theoretical physics of cosmological superstring theory. Yet, despite these achievements, as a biographer notes, "What makes Ramanujan's work so seductive is not the prospect of its use in the solution of real-world problems, but its richness, beauty and mystery — its sheer, mathematical loveliness." It was said of Ramanujan that he considered each of the first hundred integers a personal friend.

Mathematicians today would no doubt travel back in time if they could, simply to ask Ramanujan a question. I would do the same, to ask not about mathematics, but about friendship. I would ask him if numbers alone could express emotion. I would travel to April 13, 1919, one year before his death, when Europe lay in ruins after the First

World War, and when the massacre of 379 unarmed civilians by troops under British command at Amritsar had devastated India. I would ask Ramanujan which of his friends of the first 100 integers could best express the destruction, anger, and remorse of that day.

Would he choose individual numbers, or an equation? Maybe the pattern the numbers create in constellation would articulate their expression as much as their individuality. Then again, how could one divorce the structure from its substance? Every example of friendship exhibits the particular characters of the friends. In the full concrete connection of things, the characters of the things connected enter into the character of the connectivity which joins them. Maybe the selection of the second number would depend on the first, the selection of the third on the first two, and on the ensuing pattern of harmonies and dissonances that grow and multiply with each additional selection.

What if Ramanujan preferred more peaceful subject matter: the sound and the smell of rain in his childhood home of Kumbakonam, in the spring of 1897, when he was ten years old? Could he devise a formula to express the substance of that memory?

## GEOMETRY OF RAIN AND OF CLOUDS

The largest cloud extended from central Africa to South India, a distance well above the thickness of the atmosphere, to which the outer cutoff L of atmospheric turbulence is all too often assimilated. The derivation of the length area relationship generalizes easily to spatial domains bounded by fractal surfaces, and leads to the relation

$$(G\text{-area})^{1/D} \propto (G\text{-volume})^{1/3}$$

As one learns, one perceives the emergence of patterns. A partially understood pattern is more definite as to what it excludes (NO to spectacle no to virtuosity no to transformations) than as to what its completion would include. Understanding has two modes of advance, the gathering of detail within assigned pattern, and the discovery of a new pattern with its emphasis on new detail. We began with a starting point, and collected the elements of the substance of a performance, the facts of movement, text, music. We came to realize that their combined assembly, their duration, singularity, or repetition in both time and space had as much bearing on the definition of their substance as any internal characteristics we had previously ascribed to them. In fact, it often seemed that these spatiotemporal, more or less external, characteristics did the most to lend a performance its mood and emotion.

As I tried for myself to determine how exactly Lin as a director managed to enchant the material, the answer always seemed to circle back to her gentle yet merciless grasp of the pressures and patterns of time and space. As the trembling homage, Mike Walker, anchor and kabuki ghost, began to take shape into the piece we titled *How Dear to Me the Hour When Daylight Dies*, we proposed structuring that material palindromically, to reflect the formula of pilgrimage, a self-reversing journey.

$$1 + 2 + 3 + 4 + 0 - 4 - 3 - 2 - 1$$

Of course, this architecture in its purest form did not survive the process long. It broke down, hybridized, and in the end only a suggestion remained.

$$1 + 2 + 1' + 4 + 0 - 3 - 3' - 2 - 1$$

As always we needed to break our own rules, to leave space for X quantities, to invite the audience inside.

In 1998, one hundred years after the birth of Ramanujan, India and Pakistan had divided into two countries with Amritsar marking the border, and each had tested atomic bombs to use against the other. Arundhati Roy wrote an essay of protest. She, like so many writers before her, attempted to use words to dismantle bombs, and for that her homeland reviled her. In her essay, she wrote: never simplify the complex, or complicate the simple.

I was asked to write an introduction, to explain myself and to explain Goat Island. I wanted to start with that: never simplify the complex, or complicate the simple. Yet, there are no simple concepts, and upon examination, the notion of simplicity itself becomes complicated. Maybe the atomic bombs simply distracted me. Maybe when we began our little performance company, we thought a perfect performance could dismantle a bomb. Maybe we still think that. Granted, jumping around in an old gymnasium may be a questionable medium for the dismantlement of bombs. Yet somehow I find myself constantly returning to a meeting place of 1) facts, 2) mathematics, 3) the complex and the simple, 4) escape.

Escape from facts, from mathematics, from the complex and the simple. Escape from the impossibility of escape. Escape from ourselves, from the limited perspective of the individual ego. Lin, Tim, Greg, and I, along with Hijikata's ghost, began to work collaboratively in 1986. Whatever importance this event may hold seems to me now to lie in the word *and*. Who we were, when we met, how we proceeded, what we produced, all seem products of the togetherness, the conjunction. Since each of us was several, there was already quite a crowd. Our starting points, questions, structures, and arrangements allowed our crowdness to exist in concert, to make a micro-universe. Escaping our individual limitations was certainly one of our goals – and not only limitations of identity, but also of thought, imagination, history and progress. We escape our limits by listing them.

Hijikata:
*I once actually took the water dipper from the kitchen sink and secretly put it out in the field. I put it out there, thinking it was a pity for it to be in the cupboard, where the sun never shines. So I tried to show the outside scenery in the field to the water dipper.*

We have never tried to contradict ourselves, but only to allow multiplicity. Contradictions arise as well as strange harmonies. We attempt thought, and conjunctions of thoughts; process, and combinations of processes; structure, and a collection of structures – a meeting place where facts, numbers, the complex and the simple, and the possibility of escape might coexist as friends.

For those who tell us that they don't understand our work, who find it too difficult, too nonverbal, who ask us what exactly we are trying to say – this could be our answer.

> Some words speak of events.
> Other words, events make us speak.

## 4. WHAT IS AN INTRODUCTION?

### 4.1   X and questions (introduction to the introduction)

For some time I have written very short talks on various subjects. I refer to these talks as microlectures. By the time I was 37 years old, I had coincidentally compiled 37 microlectures. I submitted the collection, titled *37 microlectures*, to Routledge for publication. They accepted, but by the time they accepted, I was 39, so I proposed adding two more microlectures, and titling the book, *39 microlectures*. My newfound editor suggested that I call it *39 microlectures about performance*. I did not think the writing was really about performance. It wasn't *about* anything. Concerning aboutness, it seemed to me the microlectures circled around topics, and never discussed them directly, while always staying in the neighborhood of performance. But *39 microlectures in the neighborhood of performance* was too long a title for a book of short writing. I needed to find a word.

I thought of a young film director I had met in college, who had become a commercial success by making low-budget horror films in Detroit. Early in his Hollywood career, a producer said to him, "If you want a really big hit, you need to have an X in the title."

After recalling the parable of X, I thought of the word, "proximity." I wrote back to my editor with the title *39 microlectures: in proximity of performance*.

She then suggested I write an introduction for readers who may not know my writing or the work of Goat Island. This task presented new problems, since I have always had trouble aligning creativity with objectives. I began by asking myself a simple question.

Question: What is an introduction?
Answer: An introduction is a piece of writing that comes at the start of a book, containing facts about the book and its writer.

This exchange prompted two more questions.

Question #2: What is a fact?
Question #3: What is a book?

With these questions, I could start to write. Eventually, the process of writing provided some satisfactory answers.

Question #1: What is an introduction?
Answer #1: An introduction is a book from the outside.

Question #2: What is a fact?
Answer #2: A fact is a book from the inside.

Question #3: What is a book?
Answer #3: A book is the night.

## 4.2 A method: a worm (conclusion to the introduction)

For many years I found writing impossible, although I loved to read. The time came for me to start writing, or become very unhappy. In order to write, I needed to find a way to make writing more like reading. So I began to write as I read, slowly, extracting the lines I felt I had written, or wished I had written, or thought I might like to rewrite. Of course, this process must have been wrong somehow, even though I always footnoted and credited the sources. I think I discovered this method in the 3rd grade when I wrote a short report on earthworms. I copied my report word for word out of the encyclopedia. The teacher told me I had to rewrite the paragraph in my own words. I didn't at that time have any words that I considered my own, and still don't. So I was told to find a second book, and to mix the two together. I forced myself to rewrite the report, changing certain words and adding in other words that came from my second book. I discovered in doing this that instead of saying, "The earthworm awakes in the spring and burrows into the wet earth," I could say, "Once upon a time, an earthworm awoke in the spring and burrowed into the wet earth." I could start to make my report sound less like a report and more like an exciting tale of the supernatural. This was no doubt because my second source was Washington Irving's Rip Van Winkle. In this way I produced my first piece of writing: a hybrid, in my own words, although none of them were in fact my own. What was my own was how I read. I read the facts on earthworms with great fascination, and I read Rip Van Winkle with great fear. Life is short already. To shorten it more by accident, to awake after having slept for twenty years, can have only terrifying and sad results, especially for a child, already mistrustful of sleep, its blankness, its timelessness. One lies awake at night, brother asleep in the next bed, parents asleep in the next room. One tries to picture eternity, to position oneself on its fearful continuum. I must have wanted to disarm this fear, to dismantle it as though it were a bomb, and so I composed Rip Van Worm, a short illustrated tale of an earthworm who awoke one spring after having slept for twenty years, only to find his long white beard inhibited his ability to burrow into the wet earth.

I don't remember my teacher's reaction to this paper. By some pedagogical miracle, she must have accepted it. To this day I follow this method, more or less. I consider the entire library my rough draft. I go in search of lines to add to a paragraph. I pick up a book I feel affinity toward. I look to certain writers for certain qualities. Mostly I copy and rewrite lines, then forget where they came from, and whether I wrote them or not. I have to track them down all over again when I collect the source notes. I think the sources section of this book recognizes all the borrowed texts. I think I actually wrote the rest of the lines, but I can't be sure. Although I have aged more than twenty years in the blink of an eye, in many ways, I haven't learned a thing. Maybe I found the path to my own words in borrowing enough of the words of others. As Calvino said, "Today I will begin by copying . . ." The texts must be related somehow. After all, both Rip Van Winkle and the earthworm "awake."

### 4.3 Thanksgiving-2: An introduction is a book from the outside

When one sees a car about to run down a child, one pulls the child onto the sidewalk. Not the kindly man does that, to whom they put up monuments. Anyone pulls the child away from the car. But here many have been run down, and many pass by and do nothing of the sort. Is that because it's so many who are suffering? Should one not help them all the more because they are many? One helps them less. Even the kindly walk past and after that are as kindly as they were before walking past. The more there are suffering, then, the more natural their sufferings appear. Human beings so easily put up with existing conditions, not only with the sufferings of strangers, but also with their own.

Sometimes change begins with refusal. I had a teacher who refused to tolerate existing conditions, not only through her teaching, but also through her example, her presence, her simple place in an average classroom of an ordinary public school in a medium-sized midwestern town, known primarily as a producer of automobile parts and accessories.

How strange we are in the world, and how presumptuous our doings. We feel helpless and incongruous, each with our tiny candle in the mist. Only one response can maintain us: gratefulness. Is not all thought, as Heidegger pointed out, a form of thanksgiving?

THANK YOU TO VALUED COLLEAGUES AND FRIENDS

I owe a debt which can never be repaid to everyone who is now or has ever been a member of Goat Island performance group, especially Lin Hixson, who kept me alive, and who never blinks. People have asked me for my definition of music. This is it. It is work. In Chicago, many talented artists have worked in relative isolation and undeserved obscurity: Iris Moore, Lucky Pierre, Robert Metrick, Julie Laffin, and many more. Lawrence Steger has left us while I was writing this. That door, once opened, can never be closed.

Rabbi Mendel's hasidim asked him why he did not write a book. For a while he was silent, then he answered.

Rabbi Mendel:
*Well, let's say I have written a book. Now who is going to buy it? Our own people will buy it. But when do our people get to read a book, since all through the week they are absorbed in earning their livelihood? They will get to read it on the sabbath. And when will they get to it on a sabbath? First they have to take the ritual bath, then they must learn and pray, and then comes the sabbath meal. But after the sabbath meal is over, they have time to read. Well, suppose one of them stretches out on the sofa, takes the book, and opens it. But he is full and he feels drowsy, so he falls asleep and the book slips to the floor.*

WHAT IS AN INTRODUCTION?

Here it is a book seen from the outside. A book is only a book when seen from the outside. Seen from the inside, a book is not a book, but a train ride at night: one might glimpse a drive-in movie screen playing a film in a field. Somewhere in a laboratory all the windows have cracked, and now the inventor traces the fracture lines, thinking they might suggest the pattern of poetry. Can there be joy and laughter when always the world is ablaze? We need the introduction to see the book, to see it as a book, as one book and not as many, as one more book in a world with too many already, where each book's paper was once a different book and before that a tree, and one day might become a tree again. We have unbalanced the equation. The introduction is there to plant the book in, wait a lifetime, and read the tree it grows into.

A stranger asked a monk why he sat in front of a tree.

Monk:
*I am listening to this tree. This tree preaches zen.*

Stranger:
*I don't hear anything.*

Monk:
*KEEP LISTENING.*

### 4.4 On proximity

July 18, 1994. We arrived by train in Fribourg, Switzerland at dusk. We had waited in Geneva for ninety minutes because British Airways sent one of the *It's Shifting, Hank* trunks on a later flight. When the trunk finally arrived, we trained the two hours to Fribourg. Adrian, a young man volunteering with the festival, met us at the station. He drove Lin and the luggage in a car while the rest of us walked to Belluard Bollwerk, the three-story circular fifteenth-century fortress converted to a theater, where the festival takes place. By the time we arrived, the evening's performance by a Belgian dance group had already begun. We found the car parked with all the lugagge, but no Adrian or Lin. We looked through the small group of latecomers who, like ourselves, had been locked out. The summer sun seemed to take an hour to set in Switzerland. We walked around in the soft half light. Finally I spotted Adrian who motioned quietly for us to follow him. He led us through a stone gate into a courtyard around the side of the Bollwerk. "There is a hole where you can see," he whispered.

Lin was already on tiptoe, peering into the hole.

The three-foot thick stone walls of the fortress featured a few of these oddly placed windows, each one with a nine-inch diameter circular hole at the interior edge, tapering open to an horizontal oval, three feet wide and eighteen inches high, at the exterior edge. This shape allowed a wide field of vision for somebody looking out, but a narrow field for somebody looking in, like us. We took turns at the hole, grasping the bottom of the sill and pulling ourselves up for a view. The position and angle of the hole viewed the dance at stage level from the side, with the audience not visible off to the right. In this way we watched about ten minutes of the performance. I remember one image of two dancers in underwear with their pants down around their ankles, cigarettes hanging from the corners of their mouths, hopping in profile. Under the stage lights, from my viewpoint, they resembled a miniature moving diorama.

Many of the old cathedrals of Europe feature an architectural innovation known as the hagioscope – a small notch cut through a column which allows those standing in the side aisle to view the altar. Maybe renovators added the notch in response to unexpected overflow crowds, or maybe the notch simply resulted from bad planning which placed the column obstructing the altar view. Architecturally, the notch exteriorizes some of the participants from the ritual. The notch, a small window, mediates the ritual for those behind the column. Without the notch, the cathedral has only one space in relation to the altar, and the column simply interrupts that space. The notch creates two spaces: one in front of the column, and the second behind it. The hybrid name derives from hagio (saint) and scope (vision), a device through which one may view the saints. The hagioscope was less formally known as the squint, and the squint has a legendary double life in the form of the leper's squint, a similar feature of disputed existence. This notch sometimes appears on the south wall of a cathedral, and "lepers" or otherwise undesirable individuals, forbidden entrance, could view the ritual from that exterior vantage point by congregating at the squint. In both cases the ritual transpires in deliberate relationship to an intentional audience, and the excluded viewer, watching through the leper's squint or hagioscope, sees an unintended side view which takes in the performers, or the performers and intended audience, in profile.

On Sunday evenings as a child, I rode in the back seat of my parents' car on the way home to Jackson after the weekly family visit to the relatives in Flint. Sometimes in summer, when night had just fallen, as we drove a big sweeping curve of the highway, we would see the screen of the Lansing drive-in theater with a movie starting: the rectangular image of an actor's talking face, or maybe the quick colorful movements of a Woody Woodpecker cartoon. The rectangle looked gigantic, bigger than any movie. For a moment it appeared as a window into an impossibly lucid dimension, propped up and illuminated silently in the blue and brown stretch of field. The image flattened, distorted, and finally vanished into the empty back of the screen as our car continued past. Of that brief experience, I would think, "How unlike a movie, and how much more memorable."

Saturday, the last day of the Fribourg festival, I returned to the courtyard to watch some of the final dance concert, a duet, through the hole. Over the past week, we had unpacked our trunks, given our two performances of It's Shifting, Hank, taught a workshop, re-packed. In the morning, we would leave. Now, once again, the long Swiss sunset had begun. Four children played soccer in the dusty courtyard. The youngest, the goalie, fell and started to cry. His older brother grew impatient and hit him with the soccer ball. The mother arrived, hit the older brother, and sent him inside. The younger brother stopped crying and watched his brother's punishment in awe. Then he followed them inside, the other two kids wandered off, and the courtyard was empty again. I took a look through the hole. One or the other of the dancers, dressed in white, passed quickly through my line of vision. The rest of the time I could only see the blank lighted stage. I heard a child's voice speaking French, and turned around. Basil, the six-year-old son of the festival director, had arrived with a friend. Basil had been talking to me in French all week, not seeming to care that I didn't understand. I picked him up so he could see through the hole. Then the friend said something in French, so I put Basil down and picked up the friend.

I held the child up to the hole. I didn't know him or speak his language. We stood like that and together watched the side of the dance duet, or watched the empty stage when we couldn't see the dancers. A kind of accident, a coincidence, brought us together in that way, in proximity of a performance, with the sun going down. It lasted only a moment.

The stage became dark. Then the lights came up, and in profile the dancers bowed. Basil's friend said something in French, and I put him down. As the two of them walked away, I heard an odd, oscillating, far away sound. It was coming from the hole. The audience was applauding.

## 5. TO THE LISTENER

When listening, please bear in mind: I have tried to compose some of your most particular experiences. I realize that you may consider it impossible for one to compose the experience of another. I realize that you are not a typical, but very particular, listener. You have begun to listen in such a way that you attend only to the note being played at the moment — you try to forget a sound as soon as it stops and not to anticipate what will happen next. Your concentration lapses frequently. You are not a thorough listener, and proud of it. You have a sense that almost anything can happen next: across boundaries, with many connecting threads.

I realize that I have imagined you. Nevertheless, you have one invaluable advantage; you are the one listener about whom I really know something. You are the one I feel closest to, even if I do not know you personally. You are absolutely necessary for me — since it would be impossible for me to imagine this process other than in conjunction with a constantly imagined percipient. In this way creation and perception intermingle and are elements of the same complex phenomenon. In this way, we have begun to write this book together. Now the question arises: How do we proceed?

We proceed in absolute freedom, within certain limits: the limits of our abilities, the limits of work and play, the limits of the next ten minutes, and the limited size of my desktop; the limits of bodies, the memory of bodies, and the motion we make toward and away from our own death; the limits of justice, creativity, natural resources, blankness, the limits of space, time, sound, instability, the fractal scaling of cloudshapes, leaf veins, the circulatory system, heartbeats, the rhythms of sleep and insomnia; the limits of our skill as dancers, the limits of I need a job, the limits of the echo off the opposite wall of the Grand Canyon.

We proceed in almost any direction, across boundaries, with many connecting threads. We proceed like the mosquito that bites the iron ox. We proceed with no need to fear or to hope, but only to find new ways of understanding.

# o.  WHAT IS A MICROLECTURE?

## FIRST BOOK: BOOKMARK (1969)

I needed a bookmark. When I could no longer finish a book at one sitting (*One fish, two fish, red fish, blue fish*) it meant I had become an adult. At least I had begun to read like one. A peculiar item came into my possession, a souvenir from my parents' trip to the Jackson Harness Raceway: a betting ticket (from a losing race). It listed the horse names and start time, and I somehow resolved to write on its blank reverse side the title and author of every library book I read while using it as my bookmark. First book: *Treasure Island* by Robert Louis Stevenson. Second book, a couple of months later: *Kidnapped* by Robert Louis Stevenson. With the third book, my problems began. Despite repeated attempts I failed to read beyond the first chapter. Yet I felt determined to add it. Deciding the first chapter represented a substantial enough accomplishment, I wrote on the back of my bookmark: *Dracula* by Bram Stoker. By the fourth book, I could not read past the first page. My bookmark needed this title, yet if I added it, what then? Would my list include not books read, but simply books begun? Books checked out from the library? Nevertheless, I capitulated to my urge, and after reading only page one, I added the fourth book.

> *Treasure Island* by Robert Louis Stevenson
> *Kidnapped* by Robert Louis Stevenson
> *Dracula* by Bram Stoker
> *Frankenstein* by Mary Shelley

The back of the racing ticket – the different color inks, the clear passage of time between each entry, the world suggested by each title and the universe suggested by their juxtaposition – had become more fascinating to me than the books themselves. I suspected that in my whole life I would never read past the point at which I entered the book on the bookmark (and this has proved true). A question must have occurred to me which I could not at the time articulate, but which I now understand as this: At what point does the bookmark become the book?

## MICROLUDE (JANUARY, 1996)

I had been invited to speak at Dartington College of Arts, Devon, England, my first invitation of this kind. I had nothing to say on the topic of Performance Writing but unrelated fragments. I set my so-called writing aside to listen to my current favorite composer, György Kurtág: *Hommage to Mihály András — twelve microludes.*

We see in Kurtág's way of thinking, sentences and clauses, as it were. Kurtág himself once described this as a process in which "a statement occurs — and is then answered". On the other hand comes the extreme condensing of forms (which at times almost shades away into silence) into minute aphoristic gestures — a sigh, or a joyous breath of musical particles, frozen images: in short, sound objects rather than sound processes. Personal statements, made in the form of private confessions, become statements about the world in general; the listener is confronted with a very subjective view of the musical language. Kurtág's many movements, though not always so titled, pay homage to various individuals. It is in this light that they should be understood.

A whole fragment has its own beginning, middle and end. I wrote to Dartington that I would present a series of five microlectures.


## THE GOLDEN BOAT (APRIL 13, 1996)

Good morning. Thanks to Caroline and Ric, and all the hardworking organizers of this conference. Before I begin, I need to make some important amendments to the description of this talk in your program. First, I will not be discussing performance writing — at least not directly. Instead, through the exploration of related concepts, I will try to approach performance writing through a kind of indirect process of encirclement. This method perhaps reflects my position in Goat Island as a performer and a collaborator, and not specifically a writer. It also hopefully reflects in part the process of Goat Island — a process which values the considered response no more than and no less than the seemingly unrelated distraction or the simple mistake. Second, I still intend to deliver five microlectures, but through circumstances beyond my control, they are no longer all exactly three minutes in length — the first, third, and fifth have grown to a length of four and a half minutes. Finally, speaking here at Dartington gives me the opportunity to evoke the spirit of the Bengali writer Rabindranath Tagore, whose educational innovations in India in the first half of the twentieth century inspired the founders of this institution. In his poem "The Golden Boat" Tagore tells the story of the poor field laborer who at harvest time loads all his crops onto a boat, and then asks the boat's driver if he himself may also board. But now filled with his crops, the boat has no more room for him, and the farmer sits alone in his empty field as the boat sails away up the river. "I have nothing," he says, "the golden boat has taken all." Please think of my microlectures as this farmer's crops, and be reassured that the golden boat of time will carry each one away in less than five minutes.

## 1.1  A MISUNDERSTANDING

A few years ago, a producer whose name was Rollo made a special trip to see a performance of Goat Island's piece *It's Shifting, Hank*. Afterwards he wanted to give us his reaction, and I was elected to talk to him. I can summarize the conversation now as follows:

Rollo said: What is the reason for all this repetition?
And I said: What repetition?

Although at the moment I had no idea what he meant, I did sense that a significant insight lay somewhere at the heart of our misunderstanding.

Take for example the process of memorizing an alphabet. Is the act of recitation repetitious? One says one letter, and then another, and then another. But if all the letters are different, one could say there is no repetition. It is only at the point where a letter returns, and we recognize its return, that familiarity has occurred. But is even that a repetition? Perhaps the letter returns changed by time and events, altered by the nature of the intervening letters. At this point, can we say that there has been an occurrence of music?

To state the problem: what some see as a single moment repeating, others see as a nonrepeating series of similar moments. The difference in perception indicates not only how closely one is prepared to examine any given moment, but also a basic difference in philosophy. As John Cage said in his "Lecture on Nothing", "Repetition is only repetition if we feel that we own it." To restate the problem: does one see the repeating/nonrepeating moment as occurring *inside of* or *outside of* a language? Because with his invocation of *ownership*, Cage perhaps refers not only to possession, but also to understanding, recognition, and especially familiarity. An authority on dance, whom we may refer to as an informed viewer, upon seeing a dancer perform two similar moves, may conclude, "The dancer repeated the step." One who is ignorant of dance and claims no ownership of its language, whom we may refer to as an ecstatic viewer, at this same moment might say, "The dancer performed two similar movements – the first in one place in the room, the second a little later in a different place in the room." The differences observed by the second viewer might seem so insignificant to the first viewer that he chose to ignore them altogether, concentrating instead on the larger patterns which conform to the language of dance which he feels he owns.

At this point we must question the dancer's intention. A creative artist, just like a creative audience member, may function as informed or as ecstatic, or may switch back and forth at varying moments of the performance. But if the artist's intention is to step outside of the language to the extent that such an action is possible, and function creatively as an ecstatic over a sustained period of time, then no difference between two moments is insignificant. Stepping outside of familiar languages requires an attempt not only to generate a new language, but also to reinvent the very notion of familiarity.

The Scottish composer James MacMillan once described his style as the repetition of ideas of deliberate limitation. Through the course of the composition these elements either remain constant or gradually, integrally transform, depending on their nature. MacMillan, a spiritual composer, has related this process, in content and structure, to religious ritual. For the purposes of this series of microlectures, I will relate it to a different ritual, maybe a metaritual, between the performance and the audience. Processes of repetition and differentiation, of microelements combining and recombining to generate familiarities, leads us into a ritual of the possible occurrence of learning.

## 1.2 LEARNING TO READ

In her novel *Summer Rain*, Marguerite Duras told the story of Ernesto, the oldest of the children of a suburban family of Italian immigrants living in France. Ernesto left the school in the middle of his first lesson and refused ever to return. Later a series of events transpired in which he learned how to read.

Ernesto must have been between twelve and twenty years old. Just as he didn't know how to read, so he didn't know his own age.

In the space under the ground floor of a nearby house, a kind of shed that the people who lived there left open for the children – there, by the central heating pipes under some rubble, the smallest of the brothers found the book. He took it to Ernesto, who looked at it for a long time. It was a very thick book bound in black leather, and a hole had been burned right through it by what must have been some terribly powerful implement like a blowtorch or a red-hot iron bar. The hole was perfectly circular, and around it the rest of the book was unscathed, so it must have been possible to read what remained of each page. The children had never seen a book so cruelly treated before. The youngest brothers and sisters cried.

In the days that followed, Ernesto entered a period of silence. He would stay in the shed all afternoon, alone with the burned book.

At that point in his life Ernesto was supposed not to be able to read, but he said he'd read some of the burned book. Just like that, he said, without thinking about it, without even knowing what he was doing. And then he stopped bothering with whether he was really reading or not, or even what reading was – whether it was this or something else. At first, he said, he'd tried like this: he took the shape of a word and arbitrarily gave it a provisional meaning. Then he gave the next word another meaning, but in terms of the assumed provisional meaning of the first word. And he went on like that until the whole sentence yielded some sense. In this way he came to see that reading was a kind of continuous unfolding within his own body of a story invented by himself. And thus it seemed to him that the book was about a king who reigned in a country far away. The king was a foreigner, a very long time ago, and he spoke of chasing the wind.

Ernesto told his brothers and sisters, who said to him: "How could you have read it, stupid, when you don't know how?"

Ernesto agreed: he didn't know how he could have read the book without knowing how to read.

He took the book to a teacher who had university degrees and a definite age: thirty-eight. The teacher said that it was a story about a king.

## 1.3 W

This fragment of a retelling from Duras' *Summer Rain* concerns our problem of learning and repetition in two ways: first, it blurs the distinction between the ecstatic and the informed – Ernesto's private invented story yields the 'correct' meaning as confirmed by the teacher, but it also yields something more – the sense that the words not only mean, but also live, and effect an irreversible change on the reader. Second, the story introduces a conduit between the words and their meaning. The conduit is the body – Ernesto's body, as he comes to see reading as "a continuous unfolding within his own body" – and also the body of the book itself, burned, damaged, and scarred. Our dialectics of repetition and nonrepetition, of ecstatic and informed have begun to be replaced by a different set of concepts yielding even more possibilities – the encounter between reader and book – the interaction of the internal differences of reader and book – through a discovered ritual of learning, initiates a momentary becoming, as reader becomes book and book becomes reader – and afterwards the internal differences have changed both, through an unfolding.

I remember as a child forming a personal relationship with the alphabet one letter at a time. I had twenty-six flashcards, and one by one I'd memorize the name of the letter on each card. A B C formed the simple first triad, D E F the almost as simple second. G was the first letter of my last name, although for some reason it always reminded me of my father. Since the most dynamic and flashy characters seemed crowded at the end, I'd work backwards at times from Z Y and X – a triad so exotic its members rarely, I was told, appeared in words at all. As a memorization device for each letter presented itself, the seemingly infinite catalogue of symbols grew smaller and more manageable, and began to collect meanings, my own invented meanings as well as those apparently shared by the rest of English-speaking America.

Over the course of my learning, a pattern emerged. The names of the letters always resembled their sounds as they occurred in a word. The letter T was called T because it made a T sound, as in CAT or HAT. The letters Q and U almost always appeared together and made Q and U sounds as in QUIET or QUIT. But suddenly I encountered the problem of W.

This letter not only defied explanation, but it also presented myriad contradictions. Why was it called W? It made the sound *wah*, not the sound W. W wasn't even a sound, it was a description of the way the letter looked. If we were going to call this one W, why not call it instead *double v*? Why not call it M *upside-down*? For that matter why not call X *two crossed lines*, or O *circle*? W contradicted the pattern. Furthermore, it was the *only* letter which contradicted the pattern. Thus I found it impossible to remember.

As I stared at the flashcard W, I knew that a problem had arisen for which logic and reason provided no solution. Three choices presented themselves. I could rename W in an attempt to bring it more in line with the other letters. This was the pedantic option. I could initiate a lifelong boycott of W, and all words containing it, to protest the inconsistency. This was the rebellious option.

The third choice was the most practical, but also the most frightening. I could accept W, and change myself. I could alter my notion of the alphabet. After all, what value is there in relentless consistency? Isn't the alphabet more interesting with one letter that refuses to conform to the pattern of the other twenty-five? I could go on building words, and one day even sentences and paragraphs, using W as though it were just another letter, but all the time remembering its difference. An unfolding took place inside my body. I knew then the third choice was the road that lay ahead for me, and also I had some inkling of its consequences. I must become W.

## 1.4 PROLIFERATION AND SUFFERING

What we call learning is a process through which signs change, subject becomes object, and truth unseparates from the reality to which it refers. What we call learning may arise through a process of repetition. What we call repetition presents an instability of differences. What we call repetition presents a permeability of identities. The individual meets the collective. A repetition that touches its limit may constitute a learning. A repetition that surpasses its limit may produce a proliferation. Proliferations always threaten order. Proliferations we find in the worlds of plants, insects, geology, the subatomic universe, the sea. But among the world of humans in the twentieth century, the exemplary limitlessness has been the capacity for cruelty, for destruction, for the proliferation of suffering.

Masuji Ibuse wrote in his nonfiction novel *Black Rain* of how Mrs Iwataki searched Hiroshima for her husband August 10, 1945, two days after the atomic blast. Mrs Iwataki's recollection:

I went straight to the hospital.

Actually it was the national elementary school building, and when a sergeant who seemed to be acting as an orderly took us into the classroom we found that every inch of the floor was covered with the injured. I had no idea where my husband was. The soldier who looked like an orderly called, "Medical Reservist Iwataki! Where are you?" So I called out too, "Hiroshi! Are you here, Hiroshi?" Something seemed to grip my chest. It was difficult to breathe. There was no reply.

Then I saw a hand raised feebly. His face was swollen to twice its normal size, and his right ear was covered with gauze.

One thing struck me as strange – when one patient groaned all the others would start groaning at the same time. It was an uncanny sound. Perhaps I shouldn't say it. But it was for all the world like a chorus of frogs starting up in a paddy field.

## 1.5 MULTIPLICITY

Between repetition and proliferation, there remains a third phenomenon. It is perhaps the most pertinent phenomenon to my misunderstanding with Rollo, as stated in the first microlecture of this series. I will try to approach it through three examples.

### Example No. 1

In 1963, American composer Morton Feldman wrote a piece of music which he dedicated to his friend and fellow composer Christian Wolff. The composition might be described as two or three instruments playing two or three notes very softly for two or three hours. When listening to it, some hear repetition, others hear difference − a phenomenon possible only through the composition's severe limitations. Christian Wolff, when asked why Feldman had dedicated the piece to him, had this to say about it:

"I think what Feldman had in mind was − he'd been to Cambridge twice when I was there. The first time he met me, he came into my room. I was staying in one of the Harvard dormitories, in an old-fashioned building, old-fashioned room with a very high ceiling. And I was sitting at a desk with books all around, and my nose − I'm short-sighted − my nose very close to the paper. And he came in, and he saw me there. And then we had a very nice time. I had organized a concert in which his music was played. And then, perhaps five, six, or seven years later, again there was a concert. And Feldman again decided to come up. In those days Feldman very rarely left New York. It was very unusual for him to go anywhere. This was quite special. And my address was once again this very same place. And he knocked on my door, and there I was in exactly the same situation he had seen me in five or six years before."

### Example No. 2

If we picture our lives taking place on a calendar − a desk calendar, the kind with one date on each page, and all the pages stacked up − if we picture each day of our lives taking place on the surface of one of these pages − and we drill out and remove a core sample of this calendar at any particular moment − for example, the moment when one wakes up in the morning and gets out of bed − then we line up all these moments in a row − one could see oneself in a kind of film, each frame of which shows a different picture of one getting out of bed in the morning. In this way, one could say, "I am always waking up. I am always getting out of bed. Every time it's different. This is my life."

**Example No. 3**

This reminds me of one of the *Tales of the Hasidim* as retold by Martin Buber. A man moved to a room in a house in a new city. On his first night, he heard wedding music and the sounds of celebration from the house next door. "How wonderful," he thought, "the daughter of this house is getting married." He made this assumption because it was the custom in the small town he had come from, for the wedding to take place in the house of the bride's family. But the next night, he again heard wedding music and celebration. This time, he thought, "How strange. But there must be two daughters in this house, each married a day apart." However, the pattern continued, and he heard wedding music and celebration each day for the week. Finally his curiosity overcame him, and he knocked on the door and asked the man, "How many daughters live here anyway?" "No daughters live here," said the owner. "Then how has it come to pass that a wedding has taken place here every night this week?" The owner explained, "We rent this place out for wedding parties, and we do an excellent business." The man returned to his room next door. That night, he heard wedding music and celebration again coming from the house. "How wonderful," he thought, "to live in this world of weddings."

What is a moment? A moment consists of a small action in a small amount of time in a particular place. The moment exists inseparable from the action, the time, and the place. It is that action at that time, for that amount of time, in that place. Some philosophers might call a moment like this Being (with a capital B). What happens then when a moment repeats or nonrepeats? A recognizable pattern of time/place/action quality emerges in a perceivable proximity, with clearly shifting detail. Maybe we can now say something new has appeared: the moment has multiplied – and through its multiplicitness, it has begun to accumulate meaning, or history – an alphabetical history, a musical history. It repeats, and it does not, in conformity with its own qualities of multiplicity. In this way, the many moments become one, and the one moment becomes many.

## 2. CRITICISM

2.1   The example of glass

2.2   The example of windows

2.3   The example of rain

## 2.1 THE EXAMPLE OF GLASS

Each time we experience a work of performance, we start over almost from nothing. Despite recognizable trends, we face infinite differences – individual or cultural details, opposing traditions, idiosyncratic forms and settings, all kinds of aesthetic extremes.

Where do we begin, how do we begin, to engage a critical mind?

This question does not limit itself to performance. It relates to all art forms. In fact, it applies to all human endeavors and perceptions, from the humanities to the sciences to the practice of everyday life. Irreducible complexity seems to characterize the late twentieth century itself.

As a result, each field structures itself by propagating its own specialized vocabulary so that its practitioners might share some basic concepts. Yet each field necessarily interfaces and intersects any number of other fields, sometimes even spawning hybrid fields. Even the purist, in order to reach any depth of understanding on any given subject, must confront conflicting discourses. A serious student of performance thus might encounter the terminology of theatre, literature, music, psychology, architecture, anthropology, and biology, among other disciplines.

One might say that we face a landscape of vistas opening only onto more vistas. On the threshold of this landscape we might pause to recall the writer Isaac Babel who described his grandmother's sobering admonition when, as a child, he told her he wanted to grow up to be a writer, and she replied, "To be a writer, you must know everything."

Faced with the impossibility of the task of knowing everything, we sometimes feel the desire to reject intellectuality altogether in favor of passionate expression. Such expression may take the form of the urgently political, the assertion of a solidified identity, or the following of individual inspiration wherever it may lead. And yet even these roads, if sincerely followed lead back to the discourse of complexity.

We have no choice but to accept this terrain, with the hope of discovering its exhilarating creative possibilities. Such acceptance requires a softening of the dividing lines between traditional differences: artist and critic, passion and intellect, accessible and hermetic, success and failure.

The softening of dividing lines does not however imply the disintegration of difference. Take for example the problem of glass. What is glass? Until recently, glass was considered a mostly transparent solid. It behaved like a solid; if struck, it shattered. But then, in the ancient cathedrals of Europe, it was observed that the tops of windows let in more light than the bottoms. A simple measurement proved that a window of once uniform thickness had grown thicker at the bottom and thinner at the top. Only one explanation exists for this phenomenon. Glass flows in the direction of the pull of gravity, exhibiting the behavior of a liquid. Thus one cannot conclusively define glass without the inclusion of time. At any given moment, glass is a solid, but over a period of one thousand years, it is a liquid. The problem of glass forces us to accept the inaccuracy of the traditional distinctions of solid or liquid. While the qualities of solidity and liquidity retain their difference, glass in fact is both, depending on the duration of observation, thus proving that these two states inextricably coexist.

We must ask not only how to engage the critical mind, but also why. Any act of critical thought finds its value through fulfilling one or both of two interrelated purposes:

> 1) to cause a change;
> 2) to understand how to understand.

As creative and critical thinkers, we may find it rewarding to attempt works of criticism, which, over time, reveal themselves as works of art, thus following the example of glass.

## 2.2 THE EXAMPLE OF WINDOWS

Most critics would not contest the idea that criticism exists to cause a change. But to cause a change in what?

Rarely has a work of critical thought successfully caused a change in the artwork it addresses. If a critic sees a film one day, and writes a review the next excoriating the weakness of the lead actor's performance, that same critic could return to the theater on the third day, and, despite the conviction of his argument, encounter the actor's performance unchanged. The same holds true for countless examples: condemned paintings, ridiculed concertos, buildings of reviled design, all survive, oblivious. Yet critics continue to offer their views. What are they trying to change?

Perhaps they attempt to change the future by effecting audience perceptions. If they can convince enough people, they believe they will achieve critical mass, causing an elimination of the despised, and an encouragement of the admired. But is this an accurate assessment of events? A critique may influence the thoughts of many audience members, but in the end they will make up their own minds. And those few powerful individuals who function in a producing capacity have the option of following the will of the majority, the minority, whatever sells the most tickets, or the advice of the critic. In this equation, the critic's power seems slight. If a critic believes in his or her own power to cause a change in audience thinking, that critic lives in delusion. Any changes of this kind are peripheral effects of a more central event.

Criticism only consistently changes the critic – whether further narrowing the views of the art policeman, or incrementally expanding the horizons of the open-minded thinker. If we accept this severe limitation – that in fact the first function of criticism is to cause a change in the critic – then we may begin to act accordingly.

We may agree on the premise that each work of art is at least in part perfect, while each critic is at least in part imperfect. We may then look to each work of art not for its faults and shortcomings, but for its moments of exhilaration, in an effort to bring our own imperfections into sympathetic vibration with these moments, and thus effect a creative change in ourselves. These moments will of course be somewhat subjective, and if we don't see one immediately, we will out of respect look again, because each work contains at least one, even if it occurs by accident. We may look at the totality of the work in the light of this moment – whether it be a moment of humor or sadness, an overarching structural element, a mood, a personal association, a distraction, an honest error, anything at all that speaks to us. In this way we will treat the work of art, in the words of South African composer Kevin Volans, not as an object in this world but as a window into another world. If we can articulate one window's particular exhilaration, we may open a way to inspire a change in ourselves, so that we may value and work from these recognitions.

What I advocate is not so unusual, because if we have been trained at all, we have probably been trained to spot the negatives, and to try to improve the work by eliminating them. Given, as we have established, that criticism always changes the critic, this approach means trouble. Whatever we fix our attention on seems to multiply before our eyes. If we look for problems, we will find them everywhere. Out of concern for ourselves and our psychic well-being, let us look instead for the aspects of wonder.

If others choose to change their own thinking as an inspired result of our critical articulations, or if they decide to dismiss us as idealists, that is their business, and we will leave it to them.

But can we recognize windows to other worlds without some formal, historical, or theoretical understanding of what we are looking at? If we deepen our understanding, might we increase our chances of locating these moments? How do we deepen our understanding?

We may think of critical thought itself as a process through which we deepen our understanding. This brings us to the second proposed function of criticism, to understand how to understand.

## 2.3 THE EXAMPLE OF RAIN

How do we understand something? We understand something by approaching it. How do we approach something? We approach it from any direction. We approach it using our eyes, our ears, our noses, our intellects, our imaginations. We approach it with silence. We approach it with childhood. We use pain or embarassment. We use history. We take a safe route or a dangerous one. We discover our approach and we follow it.

In his 1968 essay 'Rain and the Rhinoceros', the American Trappist monk Thomas Merton attempted to understand Eugene Ionesco's play Rhinoceros by comparing it to the rain. Trappist monks take vows of silence. They almost never speak. In keeping with their silent life, they live in a silent place. The sound of the rain on the tin roof of his isolated monastic cabin in the Kentucky woods must have given Merton the only inspiration he needed to approach Ionesco's rhinoceros. And when the rain stopped, he heard the sound of the military airplane overhead, leaving the nearby base, on its way to Vietnam. When the airplane passed, he heard the hiss of his lantern burning. The rain provided the window to the rhinoceros, and the rhinoceros the window to the rain. The essay's analysis balances the work of art, with the work of nature, with the work of war. Merton understood critical thought as an act of contemplation, not an act of production. At the same time, he understood it to be, like all human activity, absurd. And thus he liberated his critical mind to follow whatever might cross its path. As the zen saying goes, no matter where we go, we are never far from enlightenment.

How then can we understand the rain? We can understand it as a scientist might, by studying climatic conditions and learning the Latin names for clouds. Or we may understand the rain by looking at it and how it falls – straight down, or at an angle, or lashed by the wind. Is it a light drizzly rain, or is it only a mist and hardly rain at all? Is it the kind that falls when the sun is shining just down the street? We could understand rain by examining its effects – on plants, on people, on cities. Or we may catalogue the sounds it makes on glass, on water, on stone, on metal. We could even study the moods it evokes before it has started and after it has stopped. We could not look at it directly, but rather at what it reminds us of – childhood, violence, love, tears. Who could tell us that any of these approaches to rain is not valid? And yet we would be the first to admit their absurdity.

The modernists believed that each work of art somehow outstretches interpretation, that each criticism reduces the infinite possibilities of the work, that no critique is exhaustive. I agree to the extent that the opposite is also true – each artwork reduces its critique. Only when criticism can step a little away from the artwork that fostered it will it achieve a life of its own as a way of understanding. The way a critique discovers and explores becomes as personal, intellectual, and creative as any artwork; not to offer a comprehensive analysis of the rain, but instead one singular approach to it. Thus it might return us to our first purpose, that of causing a change. If our critique of rain allows us a different rain experience, then it has caused a change, if not in the rain, at least in the critic. And as our approaches to the rain increase, so too increases our understanding of the fleeting and fragile qualities of human life. And as our ways of understanding the rain multiply, so too will we begin to see the presence of rain in even the driest of subjects. We will realize at last that our objective all along was to understand that it is always raining.

# 3. PEDAGOGY

3.1   The unlearnable

3.2   Anthem

3.3   The ceremony

## 3.1 THE UNLEARNABLE

Suppose a young person wishes to learn the alphabet.

On a favorable day, this young person journeys to the home of a chosen teacher, carrying some modest gifts along.

The student then sits respectfully in front of the teacher.

The teacher begins a three-part ritual.

First, the teacher invokes the spirit of science. Second, the teacher recites the lesson of the thirty letters of the alphabet. When this is over, before dismissing the student, the teacher requests that together they repeat a long phrase of apparently nonsense syllables, the meaning of which remains unexplained to the student. This final step is meant to cause an increase of mental ability.

As a ceremony is considered indispensable to prepare one for the study of the alphabet, it may readily be seen that higher knowledge is not imparted without serious preliminaries.

So wrote the scholarly traveller Alexandra David-Neel of learning rituals in Tibet in 1931. In many ways, we may recognize our own rituals of learning reflected in this small episode.

The first step of choosing the right day, the right teacher, and the appropriate gifts, may sound familiar to those of us who function in administrative capacities. The lesson of the alphabet itself may reflect the experience of those of us involved in the disciplines of the sciences, mathematics, and other so-called objective fields, perhaps skeptical of the ceremonial and ritualized. The ceremonial form, on the other hand, represents a kind of performance, and those of us in the arts recognize this as an aspect which we stress, in various forms and disciplines, in our classrooms. In this episode, science and art merge; science provides, as it were, the content, and art supplies the form.

But where in our Western approaches do we find a reflection of the third and final stage of the lesson, the deliberate and careful recitation of a formula with no apparent meaning or purpose? Although the author states that this phrase is meant "to cause an increase of mental ability," she does not say why or how this practice came about. She takes for granted the complexity of a phenomenon so foreign to our way of thinking that, if not for careful consideration of the passage, we might overlook it entirely.

Yet this aspect of the described learning ritual, places the meaningful in the context of the meaningless. It shows the teaching of a lesson in the light of the unteachable. It presents us with the frightening possibility that learning only takes place in the presence of the unlearnable.

## 3.2 ANTHEM

It is Friday, June 21, 1996. The members of Goat Island are teaching the first day of a three-day performance workshop with local theater artists in Zagreb, Croatia. In a few hours time, the participants, divided into small collaborative groups, have assembled rough performances using material generated from movement, sound, and writing exercises.

In the discussion following the performances, a conflict ensues.

A man with a serious but somewhat blank expression and large glasses, has told us to call him Fedja. It isn't his real name, but as Americans, we would find his real name unpronounceable.

Fedja walked into the workshop room moments before the performances were to take place. We assigned him to a group and asked that they include him. Some conversation transpired among them in Croatian. Soon an agreement seemed to have been reached. Fedja then removed a drawer from an old desk which was in the room. He cleaned the drawer with paper towels, and placed it to one side of the performance space. He removed his shoes and socks, rolled his pantlegs to mid-calf, and appeared ready to begin.

The performance started. Two women had a dialogue, two men portrayed the wind, another man portrayed a car. Fedja began to hum "The Star Spangled Banner" very loudly while repeatedly climbing into and out of the desk drawer. At times his humming completely drowned out the dialogue. After about three minutes, as the performance reached its conclusion, Fedja also concluded the song by standing in the desk drawer and bellowing, "AND HOME OF THE BRAVE."

In the discussion I ask Fedja why he had chosen to do what he did.

He explains, "I felt the performance of the two women, the wind, and the car had such a straightforward storyline, that it needed an element which did not relate at all. The audience could decide for themselves whether this element was surreal, comical, part of the story, or an absurdity."

I say to Fedja, "Given that you felt the performance needed this kind of oppositional element, how was it exactly that you arrived at the action of singing 'The Star Spangled Banner' while climbing into a desk drawer?"

Fedja replies, "I tried singing Mozart's 'Don Giovanni,' but my group told me to try something with more drama."

At this point, the conflict begins.

Sinisa, another workshop participant, who observed Fedja's performance, objects as follows: "One cannot sing an anthem in a performance of this kind, because an anthem is not a performance, but a command. An anthem commands the performer and the audience. It does not come from the inside. It comes from the outside. In fact, a performer does not sing an anthem. Instead, the anthem sings the performer."

Fedja listens with his blank expression.

Lin addresses the objection by saying, "One works toward finding levels, and building layers of meaning. Whether material comes from the inside or the outside, it all adds up to different levels of meaning."

On Saturday, June 22, day two of the Zagreb workshop, we assemble the participants into smaller groups, and instruct them to create new pieces drawn from yesterday's work in combination with photographic images that we give them. Lin has clipped these photos from newspapers over the years. Sinisa's group receives a photo of men who look like coal miners, standing, facing in one direction, each holding his left fist clenched against his left temple. Some have their mouths open.

When the pieces are presented in the afternoon, Sinisa's group, including Goran and Gabrijela, take the position of the men in the photo, holding their fists to their heads.

They begin singing "The Internationale," the communist anthem. Various interruptions prevent them from finishing the song: Gabrijela collapses, and Goran and Sinisa must lift her up and clean her ears with small cloths to revive her; Goran gets stung by an imaginary bee; Sinisa briefly transforms into a bird and flies around the room. The singing of "The Internationale" becomes an unfinishable task.

In the discussion period, I ask Sinisa how he overcame his aversion to using an anthem in a performance.

He replies, "I thought about it longer, and I thought, 'Why not?'"

"Let me explain," he continues, "In psychology, this phenomenon is called reverse projection. Fedja has a very creative mind. I see him sing an anthem. I never would have thought of this. I transform my own inability into a rule, which I then impose on his behavior to try to stop him from being so creative. I project my own shortcomings onto another. When I think about it more, I think why not use it? It's a good idea. I don't have to be so original. I'll try it myself. The men in the photo looked to me like they were singing. So I thought let's try it. After all, when we collaborate like this, we have to remember our objective, which is to create a jam."

"A jam?" I ask. "What do you mean, a jam?"

"You know," says Sinisa. "Like a traffic jam."

And suddenly Goran interjects, "Yes, we began working and we had no ideas at all. Nothing makes sense, but we keep working and nobody tells us we're doing anything wrong, and then at last something good starts to happen. We discuss our possibilities, and we say, 'What should it be? It can be anything. Should it be ball? No. Should it be car? No. Should it be Eiffel Tower? Yes!' And then everyone knows Eiffel Tower it is, but we don't know why, and we go on, and it is right. It is like a miracle."

## 3.3 THE CEREMONY

Performance, culture, and pedagogy, the three words that define this symposium, are three concepts into which we must find our own personal avenues. If we travel into any one of them far enough, I believe we will also find the other two.

Start with the biggest dictionary in the library. This is what I tell my essay-writing students. Then, if you reach the definition, you've gone too far. The really insightful part comes before that, in the form of the linguistic root. Take, for example, the word pedagogy. It shares its lineage with the obsolete Latin word *pedaticum*, which was once the term for "a toll paid for passing through a place or country."

Who paid the toll? Who collected it? How substantial was the cost? Would there be a greater toll, or a lesser one, exacted on those travelers who did not only pass through, but stopped, and stayed? These are questions even the biggest dictionary cannot answer. They are the questions posed by Dubravka Ugrešić, the contemporary writer from Zagreb, in her essay "The Confiscation of Memory", in which she wrote, "We may still pity, but it is hard for us to comprehend the true dimensions of other people's loss."

Learning to comprehend other people's loss, and calculating the cost of that comprehension, is itself a kind of pedagogy of the imagination. As the Japanese novelist Kenzaburo Oe has pointed out, "only the imagination can teach us another's pain." For there can be no learning without the presence of others. The individual does not exist, except in relation to another individual. And where we find more than one individual, we also find more than one culture. Our pedagogy – our teaching and learning – is after all part of these cultures.

Victor Weisskopf, Professor of Physics at MIT, wrote in his essay entitled 'Teaching Science', that "we must always begin by asking questions, not giving answers. In this way we contribute to the joy of insight. For science is the opposite of knowledge. Science is curiosity."

We may take Dr Weisskopf's idea further, and say science is the art of not knowing the answer. Thus, when a teacher asks a question, and a student gives an answer, there can be no incorrect, as long as there is curiosity. We might say a becoming has transpired. There is no longer teacher and student, but rather teacher-becoming-student, and student-becoming-teacher. When pedagogy becomes the toll the traveler pays for crossing into unknown territory, we might say the classroom and the world have ceased to exist, replaced by the classroom-world becoming. Where we find the becoming, we also find the occurrence of learning. The question and the answer become the question-answer becoming. It happened in a flash, a sudden downpour. It was a performance.

As the composer George Crumb has said, "I think I am a cultural maximalist, because I find Indian music as impressive in its own right as the late Beethoven quartets. The world, the universe, is teeming with life. So what's going to happen when we confront all those extraterrestrial musics?!" The ceremony of that intercultural traffic jam will certainly become a performance with pedagogical implications.

In the end, we cannot begin to comprehend the true dimensions of other people's loss without also beginning to comprehend the true dimensions of their joy. In this moving toward comprehension, we find also the joy and the loss of the very act of moving toward comprehension, starting, like a seed, when two who are different come together and ask a question, and approach a comprehension attended by the presence of the uncomprehendable. As the poet Russell Edson wrote,

> With ceremonial regret I lowered a seed into the earth . . .
> If this seed live again then so shall I.
> Which, of course, is sheer nonsense . . .

# 4. BEGINNINGS

4.1    The first chapter

4.2    The first line

4.3    The first beginning

## 4.1 THE FIRST CHAPTER

Early in life, I came to the realization that books naturally divide into two parts – Part One: the beginning of the book; and Part Two: the rest of the book. Part One usually comprises the first chapter, and maybe the first half of the second chapter. The second half of the second chapter, along with all the other chapters, make up Part Two. As a young reader, I often did not bother with Part Two at all, and devoted all my creative attention to reading and re-reading Part One.

My childhood summer days I often spent indoors. Because of severe allergies, I had difficulty opening my eyes and breathing if I ventured outdoors on clear sunny days. Rain improved matters. This led not only to a large amount of reading, but also to confusion when I would hear people use the expression, "It's a beautiful day."

Maybe I was drawn to any book's Chapter 1 because at the time I felt I was in the first chapter of my life. Or maybe, in fulfillment of a fateful pattern of odd and mundane reversals, I was simply beginning a lifelong confusion between beginnings and endings. For after all, doesn't a book's beginning mark the end of that which is not the book?

What is a book? In a documentary film made shortly before her death, French writer Marguerite Duras asked herself this question. Sitting alone before the camera in her small house, she asks, "What is a book?" And suddenly she answers herself, "A book is the night." Her own answer seems to take her by surprise, and softly she repeats it, "Yes, that's it. A book is the night." And she begins to cry.

If a book is the night, then isn't Chapter 1 the sunset? But isn't the sunset also the last chapter in the book that was the day? Or is the day not a book, but something more like a song? And when the end of the song dissolves into the start of the book, we have Chapter 1, the sunset in whose fading light the attentive reader might imagine in the convergence of two states, multiple pathways, all the time knowing there must be only one, because the book after all has been written. But longing to keep those twilight possibilities unresolved the reader refuses to cross the threshold into Chapter 2, remaining instead forever circling in Chapter 1 like Joshua, who, empowered by the word and by music halted the very sun in the sky and suspended time itself in an infinite sunset.

I am describing my experience with the novel *Dracula*. Because in those days I read Bram Stoker, not Marguerite Duras, but I only read the first chapter, and I read it many times, lingering on and rearranging my favorite lines from Jonathan Harker's journal, as he tells a story that begins when the sun goes down.

> The sun sank lower and lower behind us, and threw into strange relief the ghost-like clouds which amongst the Carpathians wind ceaselessly through the valleys.
> "It is the eve of St George's Day."
> When it grew dark he lashed his horses unmercifully.
> I was now myself looking for the conveyence which was to take me to the Count.
> A calèche with four horses drew up beside the coach. I could see from the flash of our lamps that the horses were coal-black and driven by a tall man, with a great black hat, which seemed to hide his face from us. I could only see the gleam of a pair of very bright eyes, which seemed red in the lamplight, as he turned to us.
> One of my companions whispered to another the line from Burger's "Lenore":—
>
> "For the dead travel fast."
>
> The driver helped me up with a hand which caught my arm in a grip of steel.
> Without a word he shook his reins, the horses turned, and we swept into the darkness of the Borgo Pass.
> As I looked back I saw the steam from the horses of the coach by the light of the lamps, and projected against it the figures of my late companions.
> The carriage went a hard pace straight along, then we made a complete turn and went along another straight road. It seemed to me that we were simply going over and over the same ground again.
> Suddenly, away on our left, I saw a faint flickering blue flame. The driver saw it at the same moment; he at once checked the horses, and, jumping to the ground, disappeared into the darkness. I did not know what to do, the less as the howling of the wolves grew

closer; but while I wondered the driver suddenly appeared again,
and without a word took his seat, and we resumed our journey.
I think I must have fallen asleep and kept dreaming of the incident, for it
seemed to be repeated endlessly.

As you can see, the first chapter of *Dracula*, itself looping in an endless journey, lends itself particularly well to repeated readings. And now, as I look back on that childhood journey into the book, I realize there was another ending I wished to put off. For each word read brings to an end the life of the reader who has not read the book, ushering in the life of the reader who has, and when my friends at school saw me carrying my paperback copy of *Dracula*, and asked me if I had read it, the answer I wanted to give, and that I imagined I would want to give my whole life, was, "Only the first chapter."

## 4.2 THE FIRST LINE

In September, 1980, at the age of 20 in Kalamazoo, Michigan I went on assignment from my college literary journal to interview a writer who lived up the hill named Stuart Dybek. In the interview, Stuart recited the first sentence of *One Hundred Years of Solitude* by Gabriel García Márquez:

Many years later, as he faced the firing squad, Colonel Aureliano Buendia was to remember that distant afternoon when his father took him to discover ice.

"This," said Stuart, "is one of the finest first lines ever written. It immediately gives you that sense of memory and time passing, and then it ends with the word – *ice*." As he said ice, Stuart tapped the rim of his wineglass with his fingernail, and for a moment the pinging sound hung in the air.

The afternoon's conversation at once validated and modified my childhood fascination with beginnings, for here was a published writer whose stories I admired, who had also thought about such things, but had refined the notion of beginnings to the point of zeroing in on the first sentence only. Suddenly my fixation with first chapters seemed oversized and unmanageable. But as the concept of beginnings reduced and narrowed its focus, the narrowing paradoxically produced an infinite widening of possibilities. "I always loved Billie Holiday," said Stuart, "Nobody could sing the first note of a song the way she did." Or furthermore, "Have you ever heard the music of Béla Bartók? From the very first moment, the music takes you into its own world." My head spun as forms I had never considered presented themselves in a vertiginous list of first moments.

Jorge Luis Borges had written, "My feeling is that first sentences should be long in order to tear the reader out of his everyday life and firmly lodge him in an imaginary world." As I investigated, I found first lines, whether long or short, that proved in their own way Borges' dictum of a threshold between worlds. And thus the college library became a labyrinth of first lines.

On an exceptionally hot evening early in July, a young man came out of the garret in which he lodged in S. Place, and walked slowly, as though in hesitation, towards K. Bridge.

As Gregor Samsa awoke one morning from uneasy dreams he found himself transformed in his bed into a gigantic insect.

Her doctor had told Julian's mother that she must lose twenty pounds on account of her blood pressure, so on Wednesday nights Julian had to take her downtown on the bus for a reducing class at the Y.

The writer, an old man with a white mustache, had some difficulty in getting into bed.

The Sun had not yet risen.

Call me Ishmael.

Mother, today there comes back to mind the vermilion mark at the parting of your hair, the *sari* which you used to wear, with its wide red border, and those wonderful eyes of yours, full of depth and peace.

Once upon a time and a very good time it was there was a moocow coming down along the road and this moocow that was coming down along the road met a nicens little boy named tuckoo . . . .

I shall soon be quite dead at last in spite of all.

Then, on the evening of November 3, 1982, I read what was to become for me the most fateful first line of all.

You are about to begin reading Italo Calvino's new novel, *If on a winter's night a traveler.*

Calvino, a contemporary Italian novelist, had created a book made up of ten first chapters of ten imaginary novels, written by ten imaginary authors, strung together by the intermittent story of two diligent readers who perpetually and unsuccessfully seek a second chapter, only to encounter another first. Each first chapter grows more engaging and mysterious than the last, accumulating an inexplicable sense of sadness and loss. Calvino himself distilled this mood in a ten-line poem, made up of each of the first lines of each of the first chapters, which assemble to form not only the book's table of contents, but also a complete sentence.

> If on a winter's night a traveller
> Outside the town of Malbork
> Leaning from the steep slope
> Without fear of wind or vertigo
> Looks down in the gathering shadow
> In a network of lines that enlace
> In a network of lines that intersect
> On a carpet of leaves illuminated by the moon
> Around an empty grave
> What story down there awaits its end?

I knew then that my quest for beginnings was over. In fact, until Calvino brought it to apotheosis, I hadn't even realized it was a quest. But now, the lesson was clear. Somewhere on an early road something might stop you. It is only a distraction. But the distraction grows into a fascination, and the fascination becomes a passion. Then, at last, the passion becomes your life's work. On that day of the first onset of the distraction, when there seemed to be so much future ahead, you never imagined that your work was to discover your work, and then with all your heart to give yourself to it.

Today I've been drinking instant coffee and Pet milk, and watching it snow.

This was another first line, written by Stuart Dybek that same year. As I read it the first time and arrived at the final word, *snow*, I thought of García Márquez's *ice* and Stuart's fingernail ringing his wineglass.

Marconi, inventor of the telegraph, came to believe at the end of his life that once a sound has been generated it doesn't die, but simply grows fainter and fainter, and given a sensitive enough ear and the right place to listen, one could hear it forever.

## 4.3 THE FIRST BEGINNING

The consciousness of time is inseparable from that of change. If nothing changes, then no time has passed. But while the awareness of change has always been one of the most pervasive and omnipresent features of human experience, the consciousness of time, especially in its conceptual form, appeared much later. Just as it was difficult to separate space conceptually from its concrete content, it required a considerable effort of abstraction to differentiate time from changes and events "taking place" in it. Thus, before Western thought could reify time, Western thought personified time. Time became a person dragging all things into ceaseless flux. One can readily see how this unnamed tireless laborer developed into Sisyphus, the trickster of Greek mythology, whose punishment for defeating Death was imprisonment in that same infinite present for which his entire life had been a quest. Rolling a rock up a hill only to have it roll down again, he repeats this labor forever. As writers from Camus to Enzensberger have pointed out, subsequent conceptions of time have not improved upon this image. The rebel is Sisyphus. The rock is peace. And we in his place might find ourselves of the mind of the Buddhist monk who made the famous statement, "Now that I have attained enlightenment, I'm just as miserable as I was before."

Forgive me for all this philosophy, but what I'm trying to say is, in reaching the end of our road of beginnings, we now realize that beginnings are all there is. But in that moment of realization, we also find that beginnings cease to exist, replaced by that which is unbeginnable. Rabbi Levi Yitzhak of Berditchev certainly understood this humbling thought, in the following episode described in Martin Buber's *Tales of the Hasidim — The Early Masters*.

They asked Rabbi Levi Yitzhak:
"Why is the first page number missing in all the tractates of the Babylonian Talmud?"
He replied:
"However much a man may learn, he should always remember that he has not even gotten to the first page."

But what about the practice of everyday life? In the end, we must ask ourselves how to apply this philosophy of beginnings. I will conclude with one last story to illustrate an answer. And since this story offers my favorite beginning, it is only fitting that I saved it for the end.

After the war, the temple lay in ruins. The old monk began sorting through the rubble. The young novice approached him, overwhelmed and dispirited.

"How can we ever hope to rebuild the destroyed labor of countless generations?" asked the novice.
The monk replied, "Although we may not expect ourselves to finish the work, we must never excuse ourselves from beginning."

## 5.1 TWO INVITATIONS

On a sunny morning in July, 1987, I sat up in bed, and most of my hair remained on the pillow. When I ran my hand through it more fell out, but many strands would not let go.

"Don't worry," said Lin, "We'll cut it all off."

This moment seems insignificant in comparison to the onset of symptoms that April, the diagnosis in May, the operations and months of treatments, the deaths of patients I had befriended in the ward, the slow recovery. But because of an invitation, I now realize this moment, although it occurred in the middle of the story, belongs at the beginning.

Everything we do, we do by invitation. The invitation comes either from oneself or from another person. This microlecture appears because of two invitations: the first by Brigid Murphy in 1994, the second by Anne Wilson in 1996. I have had my invitations to this world, and thus my life has been blessed. I will describe the second invitation first.

### Invitation #2: Anne Wilson
Anne Wilson did not extend her invitation to me personally, but rather to the entire world. In a piece called *an inquiry about hair* on the World Wide Web, she invited answers to the questions,

how does it feel to lose your hair?
what does it mean to cut your hair?

The questions made me remember the morning my hair fell out, and the book that Brigid Murphy never finished. Brigid's recovery had been so miraculous that she immediately found herself in demand again as a performer, and had to cancel her book project. Invitations, however, cannot be retracted, and in 1994 I wrote a short piece which I titled *Our Cancer*.

**Invitation #1: Brigid Murphy**

On my own invitation alone, for ten years, I have lacked the courage to write what I have now written. But since I have now written it, I have arrived at two conclusions.

*Conclusion One:*

Although my tumors counted exactly three, were hard as rocks and the size of a pecan, a walnut, and a box of Ohio Blue Tip matches; and Brigid Murphy's were liquid, tiny, and myriad, I must imagine a world in which two people may share the same disorder of cell reproduction — I must imagine my cancer and her cancer were really *our cancer* — otherwise my courage to write would fail.

*Conclusion Two:*

Brigid Murphy's invitation went like this.

> "Write about an event that changed you,"
> she said. "I am assembling an
> anthology."
> "An event that changed my life?" I asked.
> "No," said Brigid, "An event that
> changed you."

*Our cancer* changed my life. What changed me were the two invitations.

## 5.2 *OUR CANCER*

Two months into my hospitalization, I noticed that I could not cry. It felt as if the tears had given up. They existed inside, but lacked energy.

Lin took me outside the hospital and told me a friend, a woman we had met, undergoing treatment similar to my own, had died over the weekend. Lin told me gently, and I found this strange. Why is she acting this way? I thought. She expects me to cry. I realized then that I could not.

Six months before, this death would have elicited tears. I still felt the sadness, but distantly. I thought the cause may have been chemical, that the medicines and substances had thrown off my body's ability to secrete. But the lack persisted after my release.

I understand now that I was leaving the world. I must have been three-quarters of the way out. Where those three-quarters were, I don't know. Wherever they were, the tears were with them. My illness had pushed them over that edge, if I can call it an edge. It felt more like a position, more like folding in upon myself. From there all the events of this world seemed equally important, equally crucial.

Returning caused confusion. I noticed one day that when I should have laughed I laughed and cried at the same time. I could not distinguish the difference. I realized that the tears had begun to return, but in the form of what James Joyce called laughtears.

Dear Brigid,

As our small party waited for the table, talking among ourselves at the Greek restaurant last night, I noticed you looking at the display of fresh foods: heaps of hazelnuts, walnuts, leaves of oregano, bottles of oils on the dark wood cutting block. You watched the cook chopping up onions, and I recognized the look on your face. Events had equalized for you. You had been pulled three-quarters out of the world. I never knew you that well, but I knew you always had more life in you than I had, and I wanted to say what's happening to you is not fair, it's not time yet, and statements of that kind. But when you are leaving the world you understand that it isn't death that is strange and fearsome, but life. How is this struggling life possible? How are these people possible? How am I possible? I am not.

I thought your cancer was worse than mine, but I might be wrong. It might be the same cancer that moves among all bodies, connecting, through disease, women and men, children and elderly, heads of state and homeless, east and west, south and north,

*our cancer*

we all share in its proliferation. I have confused the curse and the blessing. I'll try to be honest. It hasn't changed my life. It has only changed my tears. They arrive with a start – nonsense, terror, tenderness – and then just as unreasonably they ebb.

It is so embarrassing to live!

I felt abandoned by everything. A great sorrow fell upon my soul. I walked across the fields without salvation. I pulled a branch from some unknown bush, broke it, and brought it to my upper lip. I understood immediately that all people are innocent. We walk thousands of years. We call the sky "sky" and the sea "sea." All things will change one day, and we too with them.

## 5.3 LEARNING HOW TO LEAVE THE WORLD

The 1959 film *Hiroshima Mon Amour*, written by Marguerite Duras, tells the story of a young woman in wartime France whose lover, a German soldier, is discovered, shot, and killed. The citizens of the town cut off the woman's hair, and lock her in a cellar. Many years later, in postwar Hiroshima, she tells the story for the first time to another lover, a Japanese architect, who listens.

I feel nothing . . . They're young . . . They cut my hair
off . . . They consider it their duty . . . You are dead . . . and
I'm far too busy suffering. Night falls. All I hear is the
snipping of the scissors on my head . . . Somehow, this
eases the pain of your death . . . My dead love is an enemy
of France.

A transgressive relationship also lies at the heart of Russell Edson's quintessentially American poem, 'A Man With a Tree on His Head'.

A man had been married to a woman's high-heeled shoe
for seven years.

He did not like to be spoken to because it confused the
hair on his head which had a tendency to become grass
when ever it tended that way, which it was anyway,
which he hid under wild flowers he let grow in his part,
hiding those under bushes growing from the back of his
head, topped finally by a cherrytree from which he ate.

If he heard a street noise he heard a street noise. If he
heard a cow moo he heard a cow moo and that settled it,
it was not a dog barking. Or was it. Or a dog learned to
speak cow. Or a cow pretending to be a dog speaking
cow – And something very much to think about.

A cloud was once in the sky as he remembers and he
looked up at it, or was it a cow barking.

In both of these literary examples emotional disequilibrium finds its emblem in the hair.

Could we then say this about hair: it locates the confusion of the public and the private? It provides the surface on which the symbolic and the imaginary merge? Could we say that hair – confused, removed, or lost – habitates the inarticulate consciousness struggling for language, or struggling to leave language behind? The phenomenon I've been referring to derives from one of Martin Buber's short *Tales of the Hasidim*.

A hasid of Rabbi Pinhas of Kinsk, a grandson of Rabbi Yerahmiel, once came into the master's room and found him lying down and playing with his watch. He was surprised because it was almost noon and the rabbi had not yet prayed. Just then Rabbi Yerahmiel said to the hasid: "You are surprised at what I am doing? But do you really know what I am doing? I am learning how to leave the world."

In winter, 1961, Yoko Ono wrote a poem in her series called 'Instruction Paintings', which serves here as a conclusion of sorts.

Hammer a nail into a mirror, a canvas, a piece of glass, wood, or metal every morning. Also, pick up a hair that came off when you combed in the morning and tie it around the hammered nail. When the surface is covered with nails, the painting ends.

## 6.1 THE CREATURE FROM THE BLACK LAGOON

How does it feel to be the only woman in a company with three
male performers?

An audience member once asked Karen Christopher this question at a Goat Island
work-in-progress discussion. I don't remember her response as much as my own
reaction. I felt the urgent need to answer the question by rephrasing it. Soon I heard
myself interjecting:

I do not consider myself a male performer. I consider myself
The Creature from the Black Lagoon.

My dissatisfaction with the question must be understood in the context of our
performance at that time, *Can't Take Johnny to the Funeral*. At various points in this piece
I saw myself as:

> one of the six simple machines
> an illustration in a figure skating manual
> The Creature from the Black Lagoon
> Hanuman the Hindu Monkey Spirit
> an autistic child
> myself at age 6
> a microphone stand
> myself in the present moment
> an emergency room doctor
> an angel in a painting by Nicolas Poussin

This represents only a partial list of my would-be identities in this particular
performance, and I know the other three performers had conceived of at least as
many for themselves. In fact, my identities only came into existence in relation to
their identities, or in relation to my sense of their identities, and only lasted as long

as the performance provided a time/space proximity for us to share. And never, I realized, did I consider among my list of identities, that of 'male performer.' In fact, I did not even understand the term. And yet, I could also ask myself, "What difference does it make how I think of myself? The question makes it clear that when people watch me, they think they are watching a 'male performer.'" Things became confusing quickly, requiring that I turn to philosophy for clarification.

Zen Buddhism teaches that what we call personality derives from five aggregates.

> Body
> Feelings
> Perceptions
> Mental Formations
> Consciousness

With each of these five aggregates come three mistakes.

> First mistake: This is mine.
> Second mistake: This is me.
> Third mistake: This is the Self.

A more correct view might be: my body is not mine; my body is not me; my body is not myself. And the same holds true for the other four aggregates. But what then is my body? My body is a first principle, a basic constituent of the universe. My body represents an intersection between my small self and the larger self of everything else, such as air, water, earth, animals, events, other people, et cetera. Several years ago I was fortunate enough to survive an illness, the treatment for which required the surgical removal of portions of the inside of my body. It became clear to me, as I regained consciousness some moments after my first operation, that:

> My body is not mine.
> My body is not me.
> My body is not my Self.

Under anaesthetic I had dreamed I was dancing for a small outdoor audience in a farmer's sunny field in Nicaragua. I found myself recreating this dance some years later in *Can't Take Johnny to the Funeral*. In this brief solo I saw myself as Hanuman the Hindu Monkey Spirit.

Performance, like dreaming, presents us with intersections. In a performance, a performer is not a single entity. Instead of a unit, a performer is an identity in motion in a particular direction. A performer is a BECOMING. I am not a "male performer," but neither am I The Creature from the Black Lagoon. I am:

> Myself BECOMING one of the six simple machines
> Myself BECOMING an illustration in a figure skating
>   manual
> Myself BECOMING The Creature from the Black Lagoon
> Myself BECOMING Hanuman the Hindu Monkey Spirit
> Myself BECOMING an autistic child
> Myself BECOMING myself at age 6
> Myself BECOMING a microphone stand
> Myself BECOMING myself in the present moment
> Myself BECOMING an emergency room doctor
> Myself BECOMING an angel in a painting by Nicolas
>   Poussin

Goat Island, a performance group now ten years old under Lin Hixson's direction, can attribute its creative survival to a series of small miracles. We may think of Goat Island as the small self, and the small miracles result from the profound influences brought about by intersections with the larger self of everything else, such as air, water, earth, animals, events, other people, et cetera. In this series of microlectures, I will try to examine in brief but precise detail, three of those profound influences from three exceptional people. Since all three of these people can be considered women, by the end I hope to have offered some insights into the topic of the day. I hope, but I can't promise. I will at least try to offer:

> a thought BECOMING an insight.

## 6.2 EVERYTHING ABOUT LIFE

It is the summer of 1984. Seventeen of us sit in a classroom on a campus outside of Los Angeles. The room is silent and full of light. Lin Hixson is there, Karen Christopher is there, and I am there. Everyone is writing. We are students in a playwrighting class taught by Maria Irene Fornes. The birth of Goat Island remains three years in the future. The idea exists unarticulated. For now, we each write a dialogue of our own invention. Irene picks up a book from the small pile of books she has brought to the workshop, and she instructs us, "Now one of your characters says to the other . . ." She opens the book at random and reads:

> "Do you really imagine you know everything about life?"

Later many of us read our dialogues aloud. In all the variations of time, place, character, conflict, tone, theme – in each of them at one point, unexpectedly, one character says to another:

"Do you really imagine you know everything about life?"

And in each dialogue, the line fits perfectly.

I cannot imagine teaching, either alone or collaboratively, without my experience as a student of Irene Fornes. In a book of interviews with women playwrights, I recently found this passage in which she describes her approach.

My Lab is a place where we do many experiments on writing. Unlike most workshops and classes that exist in universities, where you go home and write, bring your writing to class, have it read and get criticism, the Lab is all about inducing inspiration. I have never felt that criticism was the way to teach writing. In painting classes you paint *together*; you don't paint, bring your work to class and have it criticized. There is a model and everyone is working together. The important thing is to teach how to *work*, not how to criticize a finished piece. There is something about the atmosphere in a room full of people working. Each person's concentration is giving you something. Once you've experienced this phenomenon in the practice of another art form, you have a knowledge that it exists. If you've been exclusively a writer, I don't think this way of working would ever occur to you. In fact, most writers say, "I have to be alone to work." That's nonsense! They usually need to be completely alone because the other people around them are not writing. But if you experience working in a room with people who are also writing, there is no distraction. There is an exchange of energy and you know the other writers are not there for you to chat with. Even if you wanted to talk, you would be interrupting, so there is no temptation. No one is waiting for you, distracting you, and yet others are there. It has all the advantages of being alone, without the isolation.
People who come to visit The Lab are always amazed by its peacefulness and the beautiful quality of the light.

It is the spring of 1994. I am reading Albert Camus' novel *The Plague* in my living room in Chicago. Goat Island is seven years old. We are in the process of our fourth performance work, *It's Shifting, Hank*. I reach the bottom of page 129. "I've little left to learn," says Mr Tarrou, and the doctor replies:

"Do you really imagine you know everything about life?"

## 6.3 SLOW THINKING

Arriving at the World Wide Web site of Germany's Pina Bausch and the Wupperthal Dance Theatre, one finds a button marked "Videos." Clicking on this option reveals the text, "No videos are available." Which live art practitioner has not, at some time point, wished to scrap the whole notion of video documentation? Why is it that some performance works, and some aspects of all performances, translate so inaccurately to the television screen?

In *The New Dance Review*, critic Anita Finkel wrote,

Photographs distort Bausch's work. Her work as depicted in photographs is uncomely and false – 'weird,' in fact . . . Her images, ultimately twentieth century things, are fluid and cannot be captured in stills.

We expect a certain kind of stillness from a photograph. Other kinds of stillness seem strange. We expect a certain kind of motion from a television screen, namely the motion of speed. Even the idiom of slow-motion not only presents a rapidly changing image of its own, but it also by definition implies speed. Slow-motion does not capture slowness.

In his novel *A Quiet Life*, Japanese writer Kenzaburo Oe narrates through the voice of his twenty-year-old daughter Ma-Chan. In one chapter Ma-Chan discusses with her two brothers *The Stalker* by Soviet director Andrei Tarkovsky. The three of them have watched the film on late-night television while their parents were away. Ma-Chan feels intimidated by both her brothers. Her younger brother she finds brilliantly intelligent. Her older brother, who has grown up since birth with severe brain damage, possesses an unearthly understanding of sound and music, and speaks about the film's soundtrack with startling precision. She feels she cannot compete with them in the discussion, and states the following:

I don't think I have what it takes to make an overall comment. But in the grassland scene, for example, you have these people huddled together? With a host of other props placed unobtrusively at some distance from them? And this scene goes on and on. With scenes like this, I feel like I'm looking at a stage performance where you can watch each actor or actress any way you like. These scenes are good for people like me who don't think very quickly.

The scene Ma-Chan refers to occurs early in the film. In this way, it relates to composer Witold Lutoslawski's statement that the function of the first movement in his compositions is to make the audience impatient. In light of Ma-Chan's insight into Tarkovsky's film, and into her own method of perception, those who grow impatient may simply be thinking too fast. Tarkovsky's work may prove that the television screen can in fact communicate slowness, but the accompanying slowness of thought requires in individuals either: 1) slow thought by nature, 2) slow thought by practice, meaning patience; or 3) slow thought by sheer force of will, meaning courage. Most of us live in fear of slowing down our thinking, because of the possibility that if we succeed we might find that in fact nothing is happening. I guarantee this is not the case. Something is always happening. In fact, some things happen which one can only perceive with slow thinking. Thus Ma-Chan's slowness of thought, although initially seen as a personal weakness, can in fact be taken as a necessity.

In Pina Bausch's work, the performance unfolds durationally on a stage. The image repeats; the image rotates. To witness it, one must occupy the same room at the same time. One may only experience it by experiencing it. To generate such non-reproducable performative material, Bausch asks her company questions.

> "How many people or things do you know named Maria?"
> "What did you eat for Christmas dinner?"
> "How do you cry?"

The dancer's experience becomes the answer. The answer becomes the dance. The dance becomes the experience. The experience takes as long as it takes. It repeats, and it rotates, and it repeats. The experience deserves "respect" in the sense of the word's original Latin meaning, "to look twice." For, as the great slow thinker Pina Bausch has said, "We must look and look again."

## 6.4 BEAUTY

The highest responsibility of the artist is to hide beauty.

John Cage once quoted this statement in reference to the music of Morton Feldman. The statement implies that beauty, in order to be hidden, must be present. The proper attitude of the artist toward beauty might then be something like: I know it's here somewhere.

In published comments on the theatre piece *Brace Up!*, Wooster Group director Elizabeth LeCompte referred to the transformation of the actors from self to more-self. To describe the medium for this transformation one might use the word *artificial*. LeCompte quotes film director Robert Bresson.

On stage a horse or a dog that is not plaster or cardboard causes uneasiness. In the theatre, looking for truth in the real is fatal.

The "horse or dog" in question we may consider the stand-in for *the more-self*, or even for *the beautiful*. The "plaster or cardboard" represents the chosen medium of transformation, the journey from the less to the more. The corollary medium here, I might suggest, is the spoken word. In the example of *Frank Dell's The Temptation of Saint Antony*, those words included extracts from:

Ingmar Bergman's film *The Magician*
Gustave Flaubert's play *The Temptation of Saint Antony*
Geraldine Cummins's book *The Road to Immortality*
Recordings and films of performances of Lenny Bruce
Original writing by playwright James Strahs.

Although LeCompte's approach appears fundamentally deconstructive, one sees how the process of gathering, altering, and recombining texts easily lends itself to the construction of *the more-self*. The texts become a layer on the surface of the actors, and that surface then becomes *the more-self*. This may be what Gilles Deleuze meant when he spoke of, in contrast to Jung's "collective unconscious," the existence of the "constructed unconscious" and its imminence to creativity.

I think I'm a better ghost than I am a human being.

I can't repeat this line from Bergman's film *The Magician* without thinking of Ron Vawter, the actor who for so many years populated LeCompte's productions, until his AIDS-related death in 1994. Before his *death*, however, there was his *near-death* in 1986, during which he fell into a coma. At that time LeCompte, along with Wooster Group members Peyton Smith and Kate Valk, sat beside his hospital bed and read aloud for hours from the plays in which he had appeared, hoping to connect to him through the words to which he had devoted his life. After four days, Vawter suddenly awakened. Recalling again this famous story tells us exactly how much is at stake in LeCompte's work, wherein the texts, layered over *the self*, generate *the more-self*. We see the power of *the more-self* itself.

I think I'm a better ghost than I am a human being, because I am still living, but have already begun to haunt.

The ghost is always present, but the human being only appears as a result of labor. In the process is *beauty*. I know it's there somewhere.

## 6.5 BODY THROUGH WHICH THE DREAM FLOWS

I have come to the end of my discussion of women and directing, but I don't know what I have said on the subject. I do however have an idea of what I did not say. I did not say that the details I singled out arose from some innate quality that my subjects share because they are women. I also did not indicate any commonality between these methods because their practitioners are women. Nor did I say that since Goat Island's director is also a woman, that we only look to other women directors as examples, or that Lin as a woman inevitably draws from the work of other women.

So what exactly *did* I say? Maybe I didn't say anything, and am in fact only out to confuse everybody. I am after all a man speaking at a woman's conference. It's bad enough they invited a man at all, let alone a man who begins his talk by confessing that gender definitions confuse him. Perhaps I feel that if I draw enough people into the vortex of my own personal confusion, a spontaneous illusion of order will arise, and then I will no longer appear confused.

I will illustrate this point with a story. A young music student at a midwestern college signed up to study with visiting composer George Crumb for the semester. The student faithfully attended Crumb's lectures and workshops, taking in his severe and challenging ideas on aesthetics and music. In the climactic event of the residency, an ensemble premiered a new work of Crumb's, and the excited student attended the crowded concert. As the music progressed, the audience grew more and more restless, until finally, pushed beyond their tolerance limit, a few individuals began shouting their displeasure. Very quickly the protests spread and grew to near-riot proportions. Audience members stood up, calling for the music to stop, tearing their programs, and hurling objects at the stage. In the midst of this spectacle, the student suddenly spotted the composer, unrecognized by those around him in the auditorium. To the student's horror, Crumb himself was also on his feet shouting, tearing his program, and hurling objects at the stage. The next day, the student approached Crumb in amazement. "How could you publicly revile your own work in this way?" he asked. Crumb replied, "When everyone else started doing it, it just looked like so much fun."

In the discourse of Zen Buddhism, this is what's known as *enlightenment by mistake*. Through his anonymous presence among the dissatisfied audience, Crumb accidentally learned his music was not his, was not him, and was not himself.

I'll finish by quoting another composer, John Adams, who recently wrote a violin concerto, the second movement of which he titled

> Body through which the dream flows.

Adams explained that he took the line from a poem by Robert Haas because it provided an image for the entire concerto: the orchestra as the organized, delicately articulated mass of blood, tissues, and bones; the violin as the dream that flows through it.

| | |
|---|---|
| This body is not mine. | This dream is not mine. |
| This body is not me. | This dream is not me. |
| This body is not my Self. | This dream is not my Self. |

Since I began this talk with a story about my body and a dream, I may now be ready to conclude by rephrasing the question in a way that offers some order amid the confusion.

> How does the dream divide from the body;
> how does the body divide from the dream?

I can't answer. But as a performer, I know that I have my own body and my own dreams, and the bodies of others and the dreams of others. In order to continue, I need them all.

# 7. TECHNOLOGIES OF DYING

## 7.1 WHAT IS A MACHINE?

### Question #1: What is innocence?

When I was seven, in 1922, two regiments of the Polish Army "marched" across the market square of our little village. The mother said: These are soldiers. The child said: All the people around me wear different clothes — they all wear the *same grey* clothes. The mother said: They wear *uniforms. GREY.* The child said: They all carry something on their shoulders. The mother said: Those are *GUNS.* The guns kill our enemies. The child said: They all raise their legs up together! (The child shows signs of enthusiasm.) The mother said: This is a soldier's walk. They are *marching.* The child said: Other people walk the way they want to, in different directions. They all walk next to each other, one behind the other, at the same pace, in one direction. The mother said: They walk in *PATTERNS.* This is how the *ARMY* in line marched into my Poor Room of Imagination and Memory.

### Question #2: What is a machine?

In 1972 Mr Budnik taught us the six simple machines: lever, wheel, wedge, inclined plane, screw, pulley. These six, he said, generate all the others. He held a toothpick bridge contest for the entire 8th grade. Build a bridge of toothpicks and glue. Your bridge must support one brick for one week. The bridge made of the fewest toothpicks wins. Chuck was my lab partner. He designed a bridge that looked impossible, like a spiderweb: a couple of Xs at each end held the brick, and two toothpick lines spanned the gap between. It used sixteen toothpicks. My monstrous creation used fifty-four, and, like many, collapsed overnight. Chuck's held. Chuck and I went to different colleges. I lost touch after hearing he'd gotten a job before graduating. In 1982 I lived in New York. Chuck telephoned. "Where are you?" I asked. "Washington," he said. He came up for a visit. He refused coffee. Later he refused beer. "Chuck," I said, "is something wrong?" "It's my job," he said. "I'm only allowed to drink water. I work at the National Security Agency. If you know it exists, you're already suspect. I can't tell you what I do. In fact, I probably shouldn't have visited you. I'm sorry."

**Question #3: What is dying?**

A messenger arrived at a mountain hermitage. The Master interrupted the morning's lesson to hear the news. "It's about your son, sir," said the messenger. "The war has come to your home village. Your son has been killed." "Thank you," said the Master, and the messenger left. After a few moments, the novitiate monks saw that their Master was crying. Never having seen this before, they sat awestruck. Then one young monk spoke. "Master, just this morning you taught us that all life is a series of illusions. If this is true, why are you crying?" The other monks were shocked by the question's impertinence. But the master calmly answered, "It is true. All life is a series of illusions. But this particular illusion is very painful."

## 7.2 WHAT *BECOMES* A MACHINE?

*Deterritorialization* is the movement by which one leaves the territory. It is the operation of the line of flight. *Deterritorialization* may be overlaid by a compensatory *reterritorialization* obstructing the line of flight: *deterritorialization* is then said to be *negative*. Anything can serve as a *reterritorialization*, in other words, "stand for" the lost territory; one can *reterritorialize* on a being, an object, a book, an apparatus or system. For example, it is inaccurate to say that the state apparatus is *territorial*: It in fact performs a *deterritorialization*, but one immediately overlaid by *reterritorializations* on property, work, and money. One could also say the apparatus of technology *reterritorializes* on precision, efficiency, and statistics.

The belief in the moral force of the machine has its roots in Victorian constructions of the 'work ethic.' Human industry in the home, school or factory was a prized virtue in nineteenth-century Britain. Hard work, production, and precision were the aims of rational society and, increasingly, these aims were achieved more easily by machines than by mankind. As Samuel Butler pointed out in 1872, "Wherever precision is required man flies to the machine at once, as far preferable to himself."

At the start of the twentieth century, artists and architects saw in the machine an elegant freedom from the domination of the ancient classical forms. Machines, each designed as a solution to a specific problem, derived their essential structures from the principles of engineering and science. Their beauty arrived without morality.

Every tool or manufactured article has been invested with a certain amount of human intelligence in the process of its creation, and vestiges of that intelligence can always be detected in both the concept and design of the finished object. Therefore, when we attribute a degree of sentience to a machine, we may actually be responding to these traces, our feelings triggered by even the faintest signs of humanity. For contemporary theorist Bruno Latour, the machine is a transparent entity, perpetually signalling the history of the human endeavor which ensured its existence.

Technological *reterritorialization* now takes the form of the cybernetic organism, the animal or the human BECOMING the machine. From the first laboratory mouse hooked up to a syringe of vitamin fluid, to the most recent test cockroach outfitted with a microchip helmet, historians and scientists have identified a growing world of cyborgs, discerning a sharp intensification of the phenomenon as a result of the Second World War. The new industrial complex formed during that period became the model for society in the second half of the century. The image emerges of the factory as a giant cybernetic organism in which, as in the Second World War, the scientific, the military, the material, the human, the social, and the conceptual strata of production have all been complexly aligned.

The new forms resulting from this alignment revolutionized approaches to all aspects of life, public or domestic. The architect Le Corbusier said, 'The house is a machine for living in.' Concurrently, by 1945, America had also perfected a machine for dying in.

Nuclear physicist J. Robert Oppenheimer later recreated publicly the moment he and the other members of the Los Alamos team had witnessed in secret – the first successful man-made atomic explosion. In his famous statement, Oppenheimer invoked a sacred text for the appropriate image of the

humanBECOMINGmachine, and the machineBECOMINGdeity.

A few people laughed. A few people cried. Most people were silent. I remembered the line from the Hindu scripture, the Bhagavad-Gita. Vishnu is trying to persuade the prince that he should do his duty, and to impress him takes on his multi-armed form and says, "Now I am BECOME death, the destroyer of worlds." We knew the world would not be the same.

## 7.3 MEMORY OF A CLOUD

### Memory #1: cloud from the outside

In 1964, the campaign of Presidential candidate Lyndon Johnson designed a television advertisement against opposing candidate Barry Goldwater. A young girl in close-up plucks one by one the petals from a daisy while reciting a nursery rhyme. Suddenly the picture changes to a roaring mushroom cloud. Like the guillotine as characterized by M. Foucault, the atom bomb, a machine designed "for the production of rapid and discreet deaths," economized with previously unimaginable efficiency the process of human extermination. Unlike the guillotine, this device's incomprehensible technology required complex marketing to render it acceptable for television broadcast, and simpler technologies communicated its nature and power to the American people. Photographed with a silent movie camera, the cloud in at least one instance had its explosive roar added by a modified phonograph with a potentiometer-controlled motor speed, playing a slowed down recording of a waterfall. At the age of four, I learned two perhaps mistaken but simple and indelible lessons from the advertisement's dual imagery: 1) We see this cloud from high above and far away. That is why it resembles a mushroom; 2) This cloud is intricately connected to the idea of innocence.

## Memory #2: cloud from the inside

Thousands of people, the *hibakusha* – the bomb witnesses – saw this cloud from below. For them it did not resemble a mushroom. The late Dr Takashi Nagai of Nagasaki described it this way: The cloud of smoke in the sky, caused by the debris that had been sucked up, hid the rays of the sun, bringing a total darkness like an eclipse. After about three minutes, however, as this immense column of smoke and dirt grew bigger, it scattered and became less dense. And once again light and heat filtered down to the earth. Later, around three in the afternoon, large drops of black rain began to fall, the size of the tip of one's finger. When it splashed on something, it left a stain like that made by crude oil. It seemed to come from the dark cloud above us. Hibakusha writer Kamezawa Miyuki spoke of America's deception of its victims in the interests of efficiency, through the bomb's innocent means of delivery. Japanese school children had no idea that the sole parachute they saw in the sky carried the bomb that would kill them. There was no chance to revolt and escape, or to dive for cover: ignorance ensured the technology's maximum effectiveness. Their death was extremely businesslike.

## Memory #3: anthem of innocence

Contemporary cultures produce myths about themselves: the strongest media machines produce the most powerful myths. Then when the myth is established it is difficult to make out whether reality produces the cultural myth or the myth reality. By 1955 the United States had perfected its myth of the innocent – the innocent bystander, citizen, worker, politician, soldier – derived from the humanmachineBECOMING. A machine developed to address the problem of human extermination had resolved the moral questions of that extermination by removing their burden from individuals, whose participation in the system, and responsibility for it, although necessary, had incrementally shrunk beyond the vanishing point. The bomb had assumed previously human dilemmas and responsibilities, and thus had left the roles of humans, whether victims or perpetrators, statistically, mechanically, and systemically unambiguous. The bomb had become an innocence machine. And by 1955 the children of America had inherited a similarly unambiguous innocence in an image more suited to their diminutive conformity than the adult humanmachineBECOMING. They inherited the childanimalBECOMING; specifically, the child BECOMING a mouse. On October 3, 1955, the anthem of innocence made its debut.

> Come along and sing our song
> and join our family.
> M-I-C
> K-E-Y
> M-O-U-S-E

## 7.4 *TOMORROWLAND*

Fiction often has a strange way of BECOMING fact. Not long ago we produced a motion picture based on the immortal tale 20,000 *Leagues under the Sea*, featuring the famous submarine "Nautilus." According to that story the craft was powered by a magic force.

Today the tale has come true. A modern namesake of the old fairy ship – the submarine "Nautilus" of the United States Navy – has become the world's first atom-powered ship. It is proof of the useful power of the atom that will drive the machines of our atomic age.

The atom is our future. It is a subject everyone wants to understand, and so we long had plans to tell the story of the atom. In fact, we considered it so important that we embarked on several *atomic projects*.

For one, we are planning to build a Hall of Science in the TOMORROWLAND section of DISNEYLAND where we will – among other things – put up an exhibit of atomic energy. Then, our *atomic projects* at the Walt Disney Studios were two-fold: we produced a motion picture and this book, so that we could tell you this important story in full detail. Both grew together. Many illustrations appear in both, and we gave them the same title: *Our Friend the Atom*.

With our *atomic projects* we found ourselves deep in the field of nuclear physics. Of course, we don't pretend to be scientists – we are story tellers. But we combine the tools of our trade with the knowledge of experts. We even created a new Science Department at the Studio to handle projects of this kind.

The story of the atom was assigned to Dr Heinz Haber, Chief Science Consultant of our Studio. He is the author of this book and he helped us in developing our motion picture.

The story of the atom is a fascinating tale of human quest for knowledge, a story of scientific adventure and success. Atomic science has borne many fruits, and the harnessing of the atom's power is only the spectacular end result. It came about through the work of many inspired men whose ideas formed a kind of chain reaction of thoughts. These men came from all civilized nations, and from all centuries as far back as 400 BC.

Atomic science began as a positive, creative thought. It has created modern science with its many benefits for mankind. In this sense our book tries to make it clear to you that we can indeed look upon the atom as our friend.

Walt Disney, 1956

## 7.5 THE GOLEM OF PRAGUE

**Question #1: What is a machine?**
When Primo Levi encountered his first computer, he invoked a legend: centuries ago a magician-rabbi built a clay automaton with Herculean strength and blind obedience to defend the Jews of Prague from the pogroms; but it remained inanimate, until its maker slipped into its mouth a roll of parchment on which was written a verse from the Torah. At that, the clay golem roamed the streets and kept guard, but turned to stone again when the parchment was removed. I asked myself whether the builders of my apparatus knew this story: the computer has a mouth. Until I introduce the program floppy disk, it is a lifeless metallic box. When I have satisfied him, he comes alive. In his encyclopedia of imaginary creatures, Jorge Luis Borges wrote: In a book inspired by infinite wisdom, nothing can be left to chance, not even the number of words it contains or the order of the letters; thus thought the Kabbalists. They devoted themselves to the task of counting, combining, and permutating the letters of the Scriptures. One of the secrets they sought was how to create living beings. "Golem" was the name given to the man created by combinations of letters. Eleazar of Worms preserved the secret formula. The procedures involved cover twenty-three folio columns and require knowledge of the "alphabets of the 221 gates," which must be recited over each of the Golem's organs. The word *Emet*, which means "Truth," should be marked on its forehead. To destroy the creature, the first letter must be obliterated, forming the word *met*, meaning "death."

## Question #2: What is dying?

The hero of Gustav Meyrink's 1915 novel *The Golem*, lost one night in the Prague ghetto, wanders through a tunnel into a chamber. Without explanation he begins to shiver. He paces the room in a vain attempt to warm himself. "This is death," he says to himself. "The heap of rags in the corner caught my eye, and I pulled them, with shaking hands, over my own clothes. They stank of mould. I crouched in the opposite corner, feeling the warmth creep slowly back into my skin." He notices a card lying on the floor in the moonlight, and he cannot take his eyes off it. Suddenly he realizes he has wandered into the room where the Golem was once said to reside, he has dressed himself in the Golem's clothes, and the card which obsesses him is the means of the Golem's animation. He climbs to the window. "Two old women came hobbling along the street, and I half forced my head through the grating and cried to them. Once they caught sight of me, they uttered one piercing cry and fled. I knew. They had taken me for the Golem."

## Question #3: What is innocence?

Let us speak briefly about the earth. It is the ardent, eccentric, intense focal point outside the territory. The earth exists only in the movement of *Deterritorialization*. More than that, it is *Deterritorialization* itself: that is why it belongs to the Cosmos, and presents itself as the material through which human beings tap cosmic forces. We could call *Deterritorialization* the creator of the earth — a new land, a universe. The human produces the transparent entity of technology, and in return, technology offers to retransparentize the human. We must ask ourselves not only how we will USE technology, but also whether we will BECOME technology. According to the legends of the Golem, the means of the BECOMING is language. Meyrink's hero returns to his human state through the incantations of a holy man; the ghetto's wise, impoverished rabbi. What the language of technology *reterritorializes*, the language of wisdom may *deterritorialize*. In his most famous speech, Mario Savio, leader of the Berkeley Free Speech Movement of the 1960s, opened a window onto the outside of the territory. There is a time when the operation of the machine becomes so odious, makes you so sick at heart, that you can't take part. And you've got to put your bodies on the gears, and upon the wheels, upon the levers, upon all the apparatus. And you've got to make it stop. The machine we may now see as ourselves *reterritorialized*; the humanmachineBECOMING; the bodies we now see as ourselves *deterritorializing*. The language itself is the movement by which one leaves the territory, creates the earth. It is the operation of the line of flight — a new land, a universe.

# 8. HOW DOES A WORK WORK WHERE?

8.1    What is a work?

8.2    What is work?

8.3    What is where?

## 8.1 WHAT IS A WORK?

To answer the question, "How does a work work where?" we must first divide it into three subquestions: 1) What is a work? 2) What is work? and 3) What is where? Once we answer these, we may go on to the how.

### Question #1: What is a work?

A work is an object which is infinite and singular. By infinite, I mean that the singularity of the work, which allows us in fact to refer to it as a work, is itself comprised of infinite events. We can divide those events into two kinds of infinities: first the infinity of microevents on a molecular, atomic, and subatomic level, because anything which is noticeable must be made up of parts which are not; and second the infinity of macroevents, that are happening in our present, and that have happened in our past, and that clearly define a work, and temper and shape our perceptions of it, and our responses to it.

Take for example a painting. Let us attempt to view *The Conversion of St Paul* by Caravaggio. First, we must travel to Rome. Once there, we must find the Chiesa Santa Maria del Popolo. Upon entering the unlit cavernous church, we see the painting immediately, and see that we cannot see it. It hangs high on the wall obscured in shadow twenty feet away beyond an uncrossable boundary. We notice a small box to our right, labeled with the word *luce*, below which is a slot the size of a 100 lira coin. One of us volunteers to drop a coin in the slot, and suddenly a miraculous heavenly beam of electric light from the ceiling illuminates *The Conversion of St Paul* by Caravaggio. Before we can begin our contemplation, we realize that tourists from all corners of the church have swarmed to our position, it being the only illuminated area. Jostling to maintain our view of the painting, we focus our concentration on the cramped and colorful composition. We feel momentarily overwhelmed, not just by the startling structures and figures, but also by the textures. We see St Paul on his back on the ground, eyes closed and arms outstretched to an interior heaven, his horse beside him, one front hoof poised above Paul's chest, reined by a frightened steward. Above Paul's head, the horse's head; above the horse's head, the steward's head; above the steward's head just off the corner of the canvas, in the sky . . . With a click the light has gone out, plunging the painting back into darkness. The tourists hesitate, waiting for somebody to volunteer another coin. When no one does, they wander off again into the interior of the church.

What is *The Conversion of St Paul* by Caravaggio? We expected a painting, but found a series of events. Does the painting we expected exist? There is the painting, but there is also the coin box and the coin, ourselves and the crowd, the church of Santa Maria del Popolo and the city of Rome, the shadows and the light. Of course *The Conversion of St Paul* by Caravaggio exists, but this is not really the question. The question is where does *The Conversion of St Paul* by Caravaggio stop? What is a work? A work is an object overflowing its frame, converging into a series of other objects each overflowing their frames, not becoming one another, but becoming events, each moving in the direction of their own infinite singularity and difference. Somebody pulls another 100 lira coin from a pocket, holds it over the slot, and says, "Get ready."

## 8.2 WHAT IS WORK?

### Question #2: What is work?
A human being is an organism that works; this man is a unit of labor. This is not a quote from Karl Marx, but rather what I thought growing up in Flint, Michigan, before I encountered people who don't work. My grandfather, my father's father, worked in the General Motors auto plant that gave birth, in 1927, to the United Auto Workers Union as a result of the massive sit-down strike that he participated in. At the outset of our performance *How Dear to Me the Hour When Daylight Dies*, when my grandfather was 92, I contributed what for me was a homage to his years on the assembly line – a sequence in which I stood very still, lifted both arms to chest level, rubbed the back of my right hand in a circular motion with the fingers of my left hand, dropped both arms, took three breaths, and repeated the gesture. Under Lin's direction and with the input of the group, the homage took shape. After seven repetitions, I left my right hand raised, and lowered my left only. After nine repetitions of that, I left both hands raised. After twelve repetitions of that, I dropped both arms and began again. The performance of the action required considerable concentration, which I had not expected when I began devising it. As I performed it in front of an audience, in the stillness and the focus which ensued, I imagined the spirit of my grandfather descending on me, even though he was still living, and I imagined my gesture becoming a repetition of his countless gestures at work, my hands becoming his, my face becoming his. My work became the work of becoming my grandfather at work, and when his spirit joined me, it did not descend, but grew from micropoints inside me – in my hands, behind my eyes, in my arms and my

chest, and in my feet. When I articulated my intentions at a work-in-progress discussion in Colorado Springs in the fall of 1995, an elderly woman in the audience volunteered the comment that she had once worked on an assembly line, and the experience was just like that gesture. When I called my mother from Glasgow in the spring of 1996 to tell her we had successfully premiered *How Dear to Me the Hour When Daylight Dies*, she told me my grandfather had died three days earlier. He had died on the day of the first performance.

> What is work? Work is life.
> A human being is an organism that works;
> this man is a unit of labor.
> This man is free,
> not because he is determined from within,
> but because every time
> he constitutes the motive of the event that he produces.
> What he does, he does entirely,
> that being what comprises his liberty.

## 8.3 WHAT IS WHERE?

### Question #3: What is where?

Where is inside. What does inside mean? Inside means inside my car. What is my car doing? It is traveling along its own particular road. What is inside my car? I am inside my car, and since I am inside my car, I cannot perceive anything outside my car until it enters my point of view, which is inside. Thus we can say that not only am I inside my car, but in fact, everything is inside my car – the road is inside my car, *The Conversion of St Paul* by Caravaggio is inside my car, and my grandfather who built my car is inside my car. Does my car have windows? No, it is a windowless car, because how could it have windows when everything is already inside? In fact, there is no outside, there are only more windowless cars. Each one speeds along its own particular road. Each one contains everything else, including its own particular road and all the other windowless cars. But each everything inside has a certain pattern of emphasis, of clarity and obscurity, depending on the car's specific speed, direction, and point of view. In this way there are different everythings. Each car comprises a different everything. We are not speaking of closure, but of infinite convergences. The convergence of all the windowless cars of my body and mind comprise the windowless car of my self, in which everything happens. But not every everything, only my particular everything. So this is not to say that there is nothing outside of myself, but rather that every everything is inside of itself and every other everything, including me.

**Question #4: How does a work work where?**

A work is an object overflowing its frame. Work is an event in which the human participates; the human is an organism that works. A work works when it becomes an event of work. A work works when it becomes human. This becoming occurs when we realize it. Specifically, it occurs when we realize it where it occurs. It occurs inside. We do not need to find a way into a work, since the work is already inside. Instead we realize a work and its harmony with our point of view. Then it and we begin to work, and the play of work begins.

# 9.   THE KALEIDOSCOPIC SELF

## 9.1 WHAT IS A BARBARIAN?

### Question #1: Who is excluded?

Arab geographers in ancient times applied the word barbar to the people of northern Africa. The word means to talk in a noisy and confused way. By the sixteenth century the word had found its way to Europe as *barbarian*. There it came to refer to a foreigner in language and customs. For the Greeks the word retained its linguistic aspect, designating one who does not speak Greek. To understand the Roman alteration of the word's meaning, we must also understand the word *nation*. Deriving from the Latin root meaning to be born, a nation refers to an extensive aggregate of persons so closely associated by common descent, language, or history, as to form a distinct race or people, usually organized as a separate political state and occupying a definite territory. One could argue that in Roman times the notion of political unity came to ascendency over the previously held definition of a nation as linguistic. For the Romans, a barbarian meant one born and living outside the Roman Empire, its civilization, and its political state – a non-citizen. As history progressed, the term barbarian came to refer exclusively to the northern nations who overthrew the Roman Empire. Thus a nation became by definition that which it is still today – an organized state which excludes an outsider; furthermore, the outsider also represents the nation's greatest threat. Without a dangerous foreigner, there can be no nation.

### Question #2: Who is included?

The history of nations, beginning with our own, is always already presented to us in the form of a story. The story attributes the continuity of a subject to our nation. The formation of our nation thus appears as the fulfilment of a 'project' stretching over centuries, in which there are different stages and moments of coming to self-awareness, which the prejudices of the various historians will portray as more or less decisive, but which, in any case, all fit into an identical pattern: that of the self-manifestation of the national personality. Such a representation clearly constitutes a retrospective illusion. The illusion is twofold. First, it consists in believing that the generations which succeed one another over centuries on a reasonably stable territory, under a reasonably univocal designation, have handed down to each other an invariant substance. Second, it consists in believing that the process of development from which we select aspects retrospectively, so as to see ourselves as the culmination of that process, was the only one possible, that is, it represented a destiny. The illusion of national identity founds itself on the two symmetrical figures of project and destiny, and thus on a 'past' which has never been present, and which never will be.

### Question #3: Who has no beard?

Chinese Zen master Wu-men Hui-k'ai compiled the forty-eight koans of the first classic text of the Zen koan, the Wu-men-kuan, or Gateless Gate, which he published in the year 1229. Koan #4, a single sentence, reads as follows.

Wakuan said, "Why has the Western Barbarian no beard?"

Bodhidharma, the partriarch from India, brought Buddhism to China early in the sixth century. Chinese Zen painting refers to him as the Barbarian from the West and depicts him with dark brooding eyes and a black beard. The Chinese monk Wakuan who asks the question in Koan #4, one may conclude, had no beard. Thus Wakuan's question, while referring to Bodhidharma, actually refers to himself, and not only to himself, but also to everybody who is not Bodhidharma. As noted by Japanese scholar Katsuki Sekida, "Zen stories are never about other people. They are always about you."

## 9.2 THE STALWART WORDS OF GIBSON'S WALLACE

As long as a hundred of us remain alive we will never be subject to English dominion, because it is not for glory or riches or honours that we fight but for freedom alone, which no worthy man loses except with his life.

So reads the Declaration of Arbroath of 1320, stand-in manifesto not of the Scottish Independence movement, but of Christian Identity, one of the many secret societies underpinning the current proliferation of xenophobic private armies in the United States. Christian Identity believes the Scots to be "the most pure of the Aryan peoples." Once these armies rallied around the obscure novel The Turner Diaries, an apocalyptic depiction of a brutal takeover of the United States by right-wing Aryan purists. A physicist named William Pierce wrote the book under the pseudonym Andrew McDonald, and true to the false name's suggested ethnicity, groups such as Christian Identity, Pierce's National Alliance, Aryan Nations, Christian Patriots, the Ku Klux Klan, and the John Birch Society now look to a mythic Scotland for more mainstream sources of inspiration. Mel Gibson's multi-Oscar historical fantasy Braveheart has become the recruiting tool of the believers in racial purity.

As William Wallace's words emboldened Scottish serfs in the closing years of the 13th century, let the stalwart words of Gibson's Wallace embolden would-be American serfs in the closing years of the twentieth century – Freedom.

So reads a recent publication of The John Birch Society.

When I graduated from high school, I weighed 112 pounds, and I was six foot. It always bothered me that somehow I wasn't male enough. So, I think in part one of the reasons I gravitated to a hate group was it made me feel like a man. I wasn't small anymore.

So states Floyd Cochran, ex-member of Aryan Nations.

Racist organizations refuse to be designated as such, laying claim instead to the title of *nationalist* and claiming that the two notions cannot be equated. In fact the discourses of race and nation are never very far apart, if only in the form of disavowal: thus the presence of 'immigrants' on American soil becomes the cause of an 'anti-American racism'. The oscillation of the vocabulary itself suggests that the organization of nationalism into individual political movements inevitably has racism underlying it. Hannah Arendt, the twentieth century's courageous analyst of intolerance, described how totalitarianism flourishes like a secret society in broad daylight. Impervious to material reality, the totalitarian state founds itself only on the myth that it produces of itself. Propaganda erases the very difference between crime and virtue, persecutor and persecuted, reality and fantasy. The private armies of America prepare themselves for the day when they will become the public armies of America, the military aspect of a new totalitarian state. With Timothy McVeigh as their martyr, guided by the stalwart words of Gibson's Wallace, their fantasy and reality merge. The crime of the Oklahoma City bomb becomes a virtuous act, destroying hundreds of faceless servants of the old order. They look to Hollywood for the mainstream validation of their fantasies. As broad daylight begins to shine on the secret society, it does not fade away.

Nothing seems more obvious than who or what is a people. Peoples have familiar names. They seem to have long histories. Yet as one poses the open-ended question 'what are you?' to individuals presumably belonging to the same 'people', the responses will be incredibly varied. Passionate debates hinge around names. People shoot each other every day over the question of labels. And yet, the very people who do so tend to deny that the issue is complex or puzzling or indeed anything but self-evident. Floyd Cochran sought a community to solidify his unstable identity. The delusion of a solid identity, the illusion of purity, echoes an aversion to the impure – a hatred of the weak and the foreign. The delusion of a solid identity assauges the potent twofold fear, held by the individual and reinforced by so much of his social environment.

Fear #1: of the complexity of language
Fear #2: of the kaleidoscopic self

## 9.3 THE KALEIDOSCOPIC SELF

### Question #1: Glasgow or Moscow?

It is the afternoon of Thursday, July 17, 1997, at the foot of the imposing John Knox monument atop a hill of the Necropolis, the massive municipal cemetery of Glasgow, Scotland. Local artist Ross Birrell delivers a lecture designed specifically for the thirty-five participants and instructors of the second annual Goat Island Summer School. Birrell's performance work, public and ephemeral, has previously questioned aspects of physical urban reality. In his performance 'The People's Slalom,' he skied down Argyle Street as though the shopping district were a mountain. Now, with maps and diagrams in hand, he explains the ancient, mystical, electromagnetic ley lines of Glasgow, demonstrating how they align exactly with those of Moscow, a city on the exact same longitudinal plane. Inverting the Glasgow city map, he overlays it atop the Moscow subway guide, thus exposing the vast conspiracy which has for centuries depicted Glasgow and Moscow as two different cities. After a crash course in conversational Russian, he gives us each a street guide, points us in the direction of Red Square, and bids us each farewell.

### Question #2: Woman or dress?

Julie Laffin crawls down a sidewalk in Chicago in a red dress. The train of the dress follows as she crawls, unfurling like a flag. The dress extends to fifty feet, but it might be infinite. Only the body stops. When the piece has finished, the sidewalk returns to the pedestrians. The dress may hang in a gallery. But briefly we saw her crawling, we saw her face, her dress, her endless red, and we wondered: where did the woman stop and the dress start; where did the dress leave off and the red go on; where did the red end and the sidewalk begin?

### Question #3: Man or money?

For Immediate Release: At 12 noon on February 19, 1997, William Pope.L will chain himself to the door of the ATM at the entrance of Chase Bank on 42nd Street and Vanderbilt Place, across from the southwest corner of Grand Central Station in Manhattan. William Pope.L, performance artist, worker, teacher, will wear a skirt made of money. As people enter the ATM he will remove bits of the skirt and hand it to them.

ATM Piece is an attempt to bring fresh discomfort to an age old problem: *The haves* and *the have nots* and what they have to do with each other. Admission is free.

## 9.4 WAITING FOR THE BARBARIANS

> What are we waiting for, assembled in the forum?
> The barbarians are due today.

Constantine Cavafy's poem 'Waiting for the Barbarians' unfolds in questions and answers, its voice a public and collective first person plural, its time the present — the uneventful mediterranean afternoon which marked the Roman Empire's collapse. The Empire, having exhausted itself before the poem's first line, now finds definition in its only two remaining aspects: 1) all that which is not Empire — or, barbarians; and 2) all that which remains of Empire — or, waiting.

> Why isn't anything going on in the Senate?
> Why are the Senators sitting there without legislating?
> Because the barbarians are coming today.
> What's the point of Senators making laws now?
> Once the barbarians are here, they'll do the legislating.

The nation that defined itself solely in relation to the outsider depends on the outsider for its existence, and as the nation diminishes, the outsider's importance grows to eclipse the nation itself. The democracy, a government of citizens, willingly becomes a barbarocracy, a government of barbarians.

> Why did our emperor get up so early,
> and why is he sitting enthroned at the city's main gate,
> in state, wearing the crown?
> Because the barbarians are coming today
> and the emperor's waiting to receive their leader.
> He's even got a scroll to give him,
> loaded with titles, with imposing names.

> Why have our two consuls and praetors come out today
> wearing their embroidered scarlet togas?
> Why have they put on bracelets with so many amethysts,
> rings sparkling with magnificent emeralds?
> Why are they carrying elegant canes
> beautifully worked in silver and gold?

> Because the barbarians are coming today
> and things like that dazzle the barbarians.

The state has become insubstantial, no more than its most superficial totemic signifier – a color, a jewel, a list, a uniform, a flag – pure visuality. The state has become an image of the state. Its language, having lost its listener, loses its meaning. The state grows silent.

> Why don't our distinguished orators turn up as usual
> to make their speeches, say what they have to say?
> Because the barbarians are coming today
> and they're bored by rhetoric and public speaking.

The poet, born Konstantine P. Kavafis in 1863, published only one book of poetry in his lifetime. A reclusive man, he worked in the Department of Irrigation of a Greek territory of what is now Egypt. Perhaps his status as a displaced Greek citizen led him to understand the revelation so devastating to the Roman Empire that lends his poem its voice – that barbarians do not exist.

> Why this sudden bewilderment, this confusion?
> (How serious people's faces have become.)
> Why are the streets and squares emptying so rapidly,
> everyone going home lost in thought?
> Because night has fallen and the barbarians haven't come.
> And some of our men just in from the border say
> there are no barbarians any longer.

As we construct our citizens, so we construct our outsiders; as our state dissolves, so dissolve our barbarians.

> Now what's going to happen to us without barbarians?
> Those people were a kind of solution.

## 9.5 WHAT IS THE WORLD?

### Question #1: What is race?

It is the afternoon of Tuesday, August 5, 1997, at the Centre for Contemporary Arts in Glasgow. I stand in the hall, Francis McKee sits in his office, and we talk through the open door.

"Francis, have you ever written anything about race?" I ask.

"About rice?" asks Francis.

"No, race," I say.

"I'm sorry, I thought you said rice. No. I've never written anything about race. Race is too big," says Francis.

"Have you written about rice?" I ask.

"I have written about rice," says Francis. "Rice is the right size."

## Question #2: Is the world mistaken?

The other in all his or her forms gives me I. It is on the occasion of the other that I catch sight of *me*; or that I catch *me* at: reacting, choosing, refusing, accepting. It is the other who makes my portrait. Always. There is a shock that happens daily, that is up to us to manage. There is a *positive incomprehension*: the fact that the other is so very much other. Is so very much not-me. The fact that we can say to each other all the time: here, I am not like you. And luckily. The other of all sorts, is also of all diverse richness. A hierarchizing spirit rages between individuals, between people, between parties. All the time. The world is mistaken. It imagines that the other takes something from us whereas the other only brings to us, all the time.

## Question #3: What is rice?

Chinese Zen master Yuan-wu K'o-ch'in organized and finished the eleventh century 100 koan collection of Hsueh-tou Ch'ung-hsien, and published it as the second classic text of the Zen koan, the Pi-yen-lu, or Blue-green Cliff Record, in the first half of the twelfth century. The three sentences of Koan #5 relate a moment in the life of the Zen master Seppo, who lived in the eighth century.

Seppo addressed the assembly and said, "All the great world, if I pick it up with my fingertips, is found to be like a grain of rice. I throw it in front of your face, but you do not see it. Beat the drum, telling the monks to come out to work, and search for it."

# 10. THREE NOTEWORTHY DEPARTURES

10.1 Nancarrow $\times$ 3

10.2 In memoriam to Kathy Acker

10.3 Not eulogizing Lawrence Steger

## 10.1 NANCARROW x 3

### 1: Tea and stopwatch

Conlon Nancarrow died on a Sunday last month at his home in Mexico City. He was 84. I talked to a friend who had a friend who once visited Nancarrow and witnessed the player pianos playing. The friend who visited, like most people, had never heard of Nancarrow, and only went along with a friend of his who wanted to make the pilgrimage. The friend who went along found the composer very pleasant, but also a little odd, particularly when he offered them some tea, they accepted, and he timed the brewing with a stopwatch.

### 2: Exactitude (from Calvino)

I wanted to tell you of my fondness for exactitude, for geometrical forms, for symmetries, for numerical series, for all that is combinatory, for proportions; I wanted to explain the things I had written in terms of my fidelity to the idea of limits, of measure . . . But perhaps it is precisely this idea of forms that evokes the idea of the endless.

### 3: Ghost of 19 seconds

A few days after I learned of Nancarrow's death, as I attempted my annual late-summer cleaning of my study, I discovered David Murray's dusty music review, printed on the pink paper of the *Financial Times* from 1990, which had first alerted me to Nancarrow's music. I had clipped it while on Goat Island's first UK tour.

Nancarrow has spent almost 50 years as a recluse in Mexico, hand-cutting his own piano rolls to achieve perfect definition for his musical experiments – exploiting more-than-human precision to extraordinary aural ends. Many are breathtaking. Try Study 21, in which two voices in even notes pass contrariwise from very quick to heavily slow and from sluggish to a crazy cascade in 3 minutes, simple but wildly disorienting. It wouldn't be far-fetched to compare the experience with what an 18th-century listener might have felt upon encountering Bach's Art of Fugue.

I think of the final 19 seconds of the Canon X, to which the review refers, as a kind of creative utopia – not only because of their extremeness, of the 110 treble notes per second in sequence harmonizing with the 2.33 bass notes per second, but also because of a more elusive reason. Certainly Nancarrow composed more complex, beautiful, or challenging studies than 21, but these final epiphanous 19 seconds strike me as the end point of a musical life of exactitude, lived to distill the musical desires of the human and leave them embodied in the machine. Although I was sad and angry that Nancarrow's death meant a loss of new compositions, I recognized an aspect of irrelevance to it as well. He had labored most of his life to compose music beyond human performative and perceptive abilities. As he slipped out of this life last month, I pictured his pianos hammering away those insanely accelerated 19 seconds of Canon X, as if to prove that once we locate our limitations, we can also engender an ecstatic ghost who will transcend them. The ghost remains, compulsively transcending, long after we depart.

## 10.2 IN MEMORIAM TO KATHY ACKER

### 1: Survivor

I met Kathy Acker because Carol Becker's car battery died. Carol had taken care of her for the day, including a visit to the health club and Whole Foods Market, as Kathy tried to improve her strength for the evening's performance of "Pussy, King of the Pirates". Since the battery failure, Carol planned to cab to Whole Foods, where Lin and I would meet them, drive them back to the club, and jump her car, so she could take Kathy to the performance. Carol had it administrated. She called with the plan. "Kathy's better," she said, "but she keeps calling me 'darlin'. It's very odd." From Whole Foods to the club Lin and Carol rode in the back, no doubt sensing my desire to talk with Kathy. After some discussion of writing, theater, failure, Britain, the future, I said something else.

I said, "I'm a cancer survivor too."

Kathy said, "I hate that word. Survivor. You're not a survivor, darlin'."

I said, "You're right. Survivor sounds permanent, when survival is always temporary."

Kathy said, "There's more to us than cancer."

### 2: Writing life writing death

I thought of that as our first conversation. Some days later, the telephone rang, and it became our last conversation. People who witnessed her final moments said Kathy died at peace. I believe them. Rabindranath Tagore the poet from India said, "I know I will love death when it comes, for I have loved life." I want to talk about life, briefly, as writing. I think I began writing in earnest when I came to the realization that the library is my rough draft. I write by rewriting other people's words, on the humble assumption that somebody already said what I have to say better than I will ever say it. My writing involves rearranging, altering, adding to, subtracting from, the words of those who came before. I did not invent this method. I copied the idea of copying. I learned it from guess who. Chance granted me a ten minute drive with her down Halsted Street on September 20, 1997, when the low afternoon sun was shining brilliantly through breaks in clouds the way it sometimes does. Kathy said she had written a new opera called "Requiem" about her cancer experience. She planned to make it into a novel to pay her medical bills. Most say she did not live to finish that novel. Don't believe it. She has only taken a brief research trip. She plans to return soon, manuscript in hand. How else could she write about death?

### 3:    Everything is true

Airplane understood, as everyone grows to or grows up to understand, that she needed a job. For since she knew blood could drip down her legs, she knew she didn't want to live on the street where there was no medical care. The minute you know you have to have a boss, you feel fear. Vice versa. She didn't know yet she now feared. The job was easy, the boss said. People frequently ask me what my definition of writing is. This is it. It is work. That is my conclusion. Work all day, work all night, 'till there's nothin' left of life but work. I never thought I had imagination. I've never fantasized. I've used other texts, or I've used friends. I've used memories. But I've never created stories by making things up. There's nothing mysterious. When I'm writing, my mind is focused on the present. Everything is true. All that she gives, all that she is given, and still injustice has the greater part. No one will make me again, no one from this earth. No one will cover over my ashes. No one. Nothing I was, am, will be. I'm blooming, this nothing – no one's -rose. With my pistil or soul, with my stamen which fate destroyed, my center's red by means of the red word, I sang, over and over, this thorn.

# 10.3  NOT EULOGIZING LAWRENCE STEGER

We find ourselves in Vienna trying not to remember Larry. Empress Elisabeth wore only black and roamed Europe in search of an elixir to cure the madness of her cousin King Ludwig II. She asked to be tied to the ship's mast during storms. We try not to remember Larry in Vienna, where the Pestsäule (Plague Column) stands, as the guidebook says, "a towering amorphous mass of swirling clouds, saints, and cherubs." By now, October, he's been gone for nine months. Were his death a conception he'd be due for birth. He forbade eulogies at the wake, and I grew impatient with his edict and our acceptance of it. What makes last wishes sacred? We eulogize not for the dead but for us the unguided survivors. I wanted to refuse, but I remembered Sunday May 15, 1994, Queen Street Station, Glasgow, the train set to depart in 30 seconds when I took the count and came up one short: "Where's Larry? My god, he's on the platform smoking a cigarette, (looking as always stylish) he'll be left behind!" But Iris read *The Herald* insistently and hissed: "Don't look at him. He just wants attention." I trusted her and averted my eyes. The departure bell rang, the doors slid shut, the train lurched and moved, and when I looked up, there stood Larry, next to me, calmly asking how long is the ride this morning?

Yesterday on the Freyung in front of the Schottenkirche two twin sisters asked me the way to Wallner Strasse, and I guided them there with my broken German. Embarrassed to find I came from Chicago, they admitted they came from Vienna. Detailed map reader that I am, I found my way to Orson Welles' doorway on Mölkersteig, a Third Man pilgrim. As the sun went down I looked up for that shaft of window light. It didn't come. The train has departed this time without you. We've left you behind on the platform, stylish, smoking. In those last days your virus consumed you from the nervous system, and I thought of the word nervous, which never described you. You told your story only through the stories of King Ludwig II of Bavaria, and you told those stories only through the artifice of amateur pageantry (a towering amorphous mass of swirling clouds, saints, and cherubs) asking to the last: whose life was this? A self worn as surface reveals a self secluded. I wonder what you might have given us had you been allowed the age of 40. Iris tells me she's given up art forever, and I refuse to believe her, because I can't stop. We write in haphazard fashion, page after page, the memories that poison us, spontaneously, without plan or system, as intricate and crowded as an anthill. We, who feel closer to the dead than to the living, continue, concise and bloody at breakneck speed, that through the telling we might become neither martyrs nor debased nor saints, but people again like everyone else. But we do not know the names of sickness, and when we look at our memories we see they have a hole. We don't write about that. We think we choose avoidance out of reverence, but even when we write about it, we don't write about it. How can we write about an absence? We circle it, and describe the edges. This absence is your absence, a consciousness hole. I avert my eyes. Feverishly you wrote the following:

LS opens vial, pours white powder into glass with water – doesn't color it. Carries clear water in wine glass throughout the following:

> Bee pollen. No? The ashes of Gilles de Rais' burned
> victims? The snow on the caps of Ludwig's alps? It's

manipulative. (He swirls water in glass) It's fake. No one is
executed in this space. No one kills himself in the rain,
drowning in a pond of water. No one. Not when he's a
champion swimmer. That's me. But it's not me.

Dennis said it: a friend of mine dies one night, grows pale as dust in a shaft of
moonlight. You long to reach him again, all your life.

Now he and King Ludwig walk the same clouds, and when we think back on our
lives full of dead bodies and bright as heaven behind us, we ask to the last: whose
was this life? With all those baroque folds of capes and robes, words and speeches,
curtains, rain and waterfalls: a life cascades into another life. That's you. But it's not
you. And this is not a eulogy. I'm not looking. Come back.

# 11. FAILURE

## 11.1 Failure: an elegy

## 11.1   FAILURE: AN ELEGY

**20**   He fell off the back of the high platform. His chair went over and he fell over backwards. And as he was flipping in the air, it was dark, black, so he couldn't even tell how he was going to land. Once as a little boy in Fontiveros he had fallen into a pond.

**19**   The coal spent; the bucket empty; the shovel useless; the stove cold; the room freezing.

**18**   He could never live within his income. He contrived a hideout from creditors in the attic to which he would flee, drawing up the ladder. He was meticulous in his work, writing and rewriting. He could never be relied upon to do anything promptly, if ever.

**17**   Moisture has crept in between the plaster and the paint, causing the paint to flake off the wall, and peeling it away to such a degree that the image has almost completely disappeared.

**16**   We design our cities, but who will design their decay? We desire the permanence of the most frivolous item, and we desire the performance of instability. Through a revolutionary process of erasure, we establish a conceptual Nevada. But what if a mistake simply reverses an earlier mistake?

**15**   A water main installed in 1915 broke in 1983 in midtown Manhattan and flooded an underground power station, causing a fire. The failure of six transformers interrupted electrical service for several days; the same days of the year that ten thousand buyers from across the country visited New York's garment district to purchase the next season's lines. The area covered by the blackout included the blocks containing the showrooms of the clothing industry. Financial losses due to disrupted business were put in the millions.

14    Unknown to us, a little piece of scotch tape had been lodged in the camera gate all day, and when the film came back from the developing laboratory, we saw the imprint of the transparent tape halfway up the lefthand side of the screen throughout the footage.

13    The Globe Theatre burned down on June 29, 1613; the Royal Opera Covent Garden burned down on March 5, 1856; The Savoy Theatre burned down on February 12, 1990. The craft apparently crashed in the New Mexico desert on July 3, 1947.

12    The cellos were doing what the trombones should have been doing.

11    President George Bush recognized the power of the supermarket tabloids. "I am especially grateful for the support of all at Globe Communications for our efforts in the Persian Gulf," he wrote to editorial director Phil Burton. "It's important that our courageous troops face this historic challenge knowing that they have the support of millions of people around the world." During the war, *The National Enquirer*, a Globe publication, had reported that Saddam Hussein tortured and killed household pets, illustrating the story with a photo of him strangling a Siamese cat.

10    Failure: accident, mistake, weakness, inability, incorrect method, uselessness, incompatibility, embarrassment, confusion, redundancy, incoherence, unrecognizability, absurdity, invisibility, impermanence, decay, instability, forgetability, disappearance.

9    Criswell was a newscaster in New York. One day the station gave him the signal that the news wires had failed. He had fifteen minutes to fill. He said, "Since we don't have any more news, I predict that what's going to happen tomorrow is this," and he predicted a piece of news that happened.

8    One should not utter absurdities lightly.

7    The failure of the San Francisquito dam in 1928 released the entire contents of the reservoir which flooded the Santa Clara River Valley including the towns of Piru, Fillmore, and Santa Paula, with an initial wall of water 200 feet high, that washed out to sea at Ventura, 55 miles away. Four hundred and fifty people died. William Mulholland, Chief Engineer of the City of Los Angeles, had inspected the dam twelve hours before the disaster, and declared it safe. He retired soon after the accident, and stated that he envied the dead.

6    Quests end in failure. One answer undoes another. Trust absence. Only fragments are accurate. Once as a little girl she couldn't get the word butterfly so tried to get the word moth.

5    The "obvious errors" mentioned above are inherent in the process.

4    The new technologies convey a certain type of accident, one that is no longer local and precisely situated, like the sinking of the *Titanic* or the derailment of a train, but *general*, an accident that immediately affects the entire world. This situation has no reference. We don't know yet what an integral accident could be, an accident that would involve everyone at the same time.

3    Jim did the countdown from 20 without stopping or slowing down. Always something went wrong, and Dave yelled the problem: fuel leak! oxygen tank! meteor shower! fire! I had to fix things before Jim got to zero and the rocket ship took off.

2    Although by its nature the noise in telephone lines was random, it always came in clusters. The more closely they looked at the error clusters, the more complicated the patterns seemed to be. Contrary to intuition, they could never find a time during which errors were scattered continuously. Within any burst of errors, no matter how short, they always found completely error-free periods. Furthermore, a consistent geometric relationship existed between the bursts of errors and the spaces of clean transmission. On scales of an hour or a second, the proportion of error-free periods to error-ridden periods remained constant. For mathematical reasons ($Dt = 0$) the set produced by the equation was called "dust."

1    He heard her prayer. Within two years she too was ill with a complaint from which she suffered for the next three years. It was no less painful or hard to bear.

0    Of this she will not speak.

## oo. TO THE READER-2

By now you must be tired of reading and ready to turn off your light. But wait.
The writer has something more to say, to postpone a bit longer the moment of
leaving. He restates his intention, retroactively. Some books, full of opinions, resemble
umbrellas. Others, full of questions, are more like rain. Why not end with poetry?
Something like the following:

> Now I give back the keys to my door, and I give up all claims to my house.
> I don't remember the moment of my birth.
> I do remember one morning when the light and smell of rain made me
>     feel I was not a stranger in the world.
> When we worked together, I never questioned you, or who you were. I did
>     not feel shy or afraid. I had an abundance of confidence.
> Now our time together has ended, and I notice how the world bends down
>     to look at your feet, and all the stars in the night sky.
> Let the things I longed for and the things I received pass me by.
> Your questions guided me. They composed my paths.
> It's April and the clouds fill up with rain.
> Flocks of homesick geese fly.
> All my questions gather into a river heading for the sea.
> Ask another.

But this poetry belongs to an earlier time. We do not desire its return. What I have put
into words is no longer my possession, and those words, like the rest, are not my
own. I would rather simply thank you for paying attention. Because of you, these
thoughts have become words, these words have become pages, these pages have
become this book, which you hold in your hand, which you have almost finished.

SOURCE NOTES

# INTRODUCTION TO SOURCE NOTES

I have been guided in my approach to compiling these source notes by Anthony Grafton's history of the footnote, with its historical enumeration of the possibilities of scholarly parallel commentary. We may consider the hypertext a recent technological innovation, but the idea that a text may contain multiple branching texts through the references layered in its fabric appears as old as writing itself. Since "no one can ever exhaust the range of sources relevant to a problem – much less quote all of them in a note," (Grafton 1997: 16) I have tried to approach these source notes as a creative way of tracking "the movement of thought" (Grafton 1997: 21). On page 29, Grafton gives the example of Johannes Kepler, who "wrote a formal commentary in middle age on his first book, the *Mysterium cosmographicum*, in order to explain to readers in a distant future the personal circumstances and particular experiences that had given that book its shape and content." Readers who take part in the work – participatory readers (Grafton 1997: 51) may look to this section to locate the production of the work "in time and space, emphasizing the limited horizons and opportunities of its author, rather than those of its reader . . ." (Grafton 1997: 32).

## 1. TO THE READER-1

Early writers used beech bark paper, or even inscribed on trees.

> *Oxford English Dictionary* on 'writing'.

❖

Sometimes time itself seems to threaten to disappear.

> . . . we certainly are living in a time, and a
> geography, dominated by radical change. So
> radical that the pace of time is increasing to such
> a degree that time seems to be threatening to
> disappear.

> Kathy Acker, *Bodies of Work*, London, Serpent's Tail, 1997, p. viii.

❖

Consider this book like an interrupted performance.

> Ron Vawter:
> In the Trilogy I took a lot of pleasure from
> performing in a new way. I saw myself as a
> stand-in, or surrogate, not playing a role so much
> as standing in for people that Spalding wanted to
> have in the same room, in the scene.
> David Savran:
> Like, in Rumstick Road, his father or
> grandmother.
> Ron Vawter:
> Yes. But I never tried to act older, or like I
> thought his father would be. I always saw myself
> as a surrogate who, in the absence of anyone
> else, would stand in for him. And even now,

when I'm in front of an audience and I feel good,
I hearken back to that feeling, that I'm standing
in for them. Anybody might as easily be up
there, but I'm the one who happens to be there at
that moment. That's the feeling I have about any
character I play, that I'm there in place of the real
thing or of anyone who's watching it. And that
makes me feel very generous, very energized.
This feeling came out of the Trilogy because I
behaved in those pieces in place of people who
were important in Spalding's life, or members
of his family. So I always had the feeling, not so
much of inhabiting an imaginative world of my
own, but of being a theatrical "stand-in."

David Savran, *Breaking the Rules: The Wooster Group*, New York, Theatre
Communications Group, 1986, p. 114.

❖

In order to fulfill those intentions, I will not imitate them, but only point to them.
On the topic of pointing, see Introduction to the Index.

❖

This section, "To the reader", owes a debt to two introductory passages masterfully
written in direct address form.

You are about to begin reading Italo Calvino's
new novel, *If on a winter's night a traveler*.
Relax. Concentrate.

Italo Calvino, *If on a winter's night a traveler*, trans. William Weaver, New York,
Harcourt Brace Jovanovich, 1981, p. 3.

Brothers and sisters, please read *The Diamond
that Cuts through Illusion* with a serene mind, a
mind free from views.

Thich Nhat Hanh, *The Diamond that Cuts through Illusion — Commentaries on the
Prajnaparamita Diamond Sutra*, Berkeley, Parallax, 1992, Introduction.

❖ ❖ ❖

### 2.1. The open book

Existence is not infinity, but that which allows the existant to be thought of as deriving from infinity.

> Harmonic unity is not that of infinity, but that
> which allows the existant to be thought of as
> deriving from infinity; it is a numerical unity
> insofar as it envelops a multiplicity ("to exist
> means nothing other than to be harmonic"); it is
> extended into the affective domain insofar as the
> senses apprehend it aesthetically, in confusion.

Gilles Deleuze, *The Fold – Leibniz and the Baroque*, trans. Tom Conley, Minneapolis, University of Minnesota Press, 1993, p. 128.

❖

There, below the bottom shelf of the theatre section, I found a cardboard box containing back issues of the *Tulane Drama Review*. I read about Bertolt Brecht, Julian Beck and Judith Malina, Joseph Chaikin, Happenings . . . I studied the photographs of Richard Foreman's Ontological-Hysteric Theatre . . .

I cannot reconstruct these references with any precision, but I believe I read T13, the first Brecht issue; T43, on The Living Theatre (Beck and Malina) and Joseph Chaikin; and T62, on The Living Theatre and Richard Foreman, as well as the famous Happenings issue from 1965, which has since been reprinted as *Happenings and Other Acts*, edited by Mariellen R. Sandford. *The Tulane Drama Review* became *The Drama Review*, which MIT Press Journals now publishes.

❖

The film society screened Werner Herzog's *Every Man for Himself and God Against All*. Kaspar Hauser has been stabbed. With blood spreading on the front of his shirt, he walks quickly through a garden, his upper body stiff and leaning back, a young boy leading him by the hand.

Werner Herzog, *Every Man for Himself and God Against All – The Mystery of Kaspar Hauser*, film, 1974.

I performed a version of this movement while wearing the bloodshirt (a white shirt stained with stage blood) near the end of the Goat Island performance *How Dear to Me the Hour When Daylight Dies*. The creation of this performance began with a research trip to the Croagh Patrick pilgrimage in County Mayo, Ireland, images of which appear briefly in a vision scene near the end of Herzog's film.

❖

My distracting embarrassment, one might say, moved to center stage.

> Occasionally there'd be lines I found
> embarrassing, that seemed especially juvenile,
> and I'd cut them. But when we went into
> rehearsals I'd miss them. I'd realize those lines
> were the strongest and most personal – and I had
> to face up to the fact that they did come from my
> most genuine instincts. So I would restore them
> and stage them as the absolute center of the
> scene.

Richard Foreman, 'Foundations for a Theater,' *Unbalancing Acts – Foundations for a Theater*, New York, Pantheon, 1992, p. 10.

❖

Consider the performance of the elevator.

> The role the elevator plays in a building of such
> enormous scale and its revolutionary potential
> make it a very dangerous instrument for
> architects. It completely undermines, annihilates,
> and ridicules an enormous part of our
> architectural abilities. It ridicules our
> compositional instincts, annihilates our
> education, and undermines the doctrine that there
> must always be an architectural means to shape
> transitions. The great achievement of the elevator
> is its ability to mechanically establish connections
> within a building without any recourse to
> architecture. Where architecture, in order to make
> connections, has to go through incredibly
> complicated gestures, the elevator simply
> ridicules, bypassing all knowledge, and
> establishing connections mechanically.

Rem Koolhaas, 'Lecture 1/21/91', *Conversations with Students*, New York, Princeton, 1996, pp. 16–17.

❖

I found a record: Béla Bartók's Concerto for Orchestra . . .

> Béla Bartók, *Concerto for Orchestra*, written for the Koussevitzky Music Foundation in memory of Mrs Natalie Koussevitzky, first performance, Boston, 1 December 1944, Boston Symphony Orchestra, Serge Koussevitzky conducting, 1943.

❖

. . . played by the Israel Philharmonic, conducted by Zubin Mehta . . .

> Béla Bartók, *Concerto for Orchestra*, Israel Philharmonic Orchestra, Zubin Mehta conducting, London and New York, Decca Records, 1976.

❖

. . . in a brown record jacket with a reproduction of a painting by Paul Klee called *The Open Book*.

> Paul Klee, *The Open Book*, The Solomon R. Guggenheim Museum, New York, 1930.

❖

What man has inflicted on man, in very recent times – the sum and potential of human behavior – presses on the brain with a new kind of darkness.

> We cannot pretend that atrocity, in the words of George Steiner, "is irrelevant to the responsible life of the imagination. What man has inflicted on man, in very recent times, has affected the writer's primary material – the sum and *potential* of human behavior – and it presses on the brain with a new darkness."

> John Whittier Treat, *Writing Ground Zero – Japanese Literature and the Atomic Bomb*, Chicago, University of Chicago, 1995, p. 18.

Treat attributes Steiner's statement to Lawrence Langer, who quotes it in *The Holocaust and the Literary Imagination*.

❖

An open book is also night.

> Marguerite Duras, 'Writing', *Writing*, trans. M. Polizzotti, Cambridge, Lumen, 1998, p. 14.

❖

## 2.2 Where there is wind

I extracted the *India Today* report, with minor editing, from Arundhati Roy's quotation of it.

> Arundhati Roy, 'The End of Imagination', *The Cost of Living*, New York, Random House, 1999.

❖

The extract of Oppenheimer's famous speech derives from the NBC News archives, Washington. I transcribed and arranged this version from the sampling used by Jocelyn Pook in her composition 'Oppenheimer', from *Deluge*. See also microlecture 7.2.

❖

The difference of the world, in the twentieth century's second half, has been, like Krishna's many forms, a series of repetitions. The blast in the New Mexico desert marked the beginning of this endlessness.

I owe much of the analysis and tone of this passage to John Whittier Treat's brilliant and thorough discussion of Hiroshima and Nagasaki in *Writing Ground Zero*. I have tried to acknowledge the extracted words and phrases as precisely as possible. The performative destruction of these two cities has remained the dominant mode for much of the US's (non-covert) military engagement. Of the bombardments listed below, to my understanding only the war against Iraq employed nuclear weaponry (in the form of depleted uranium shells). Yet the ongoing threat and costs of nuclear proliferation (as discussed in *Atomic Audit*, edited by Stephen Schwartz) also motivated my emphasis in this passage.

The record of countries bombarded by the United States since the end of the Second World War includes the following: China 1945–46, 1950–53; Korea 1950–53; Guatamala 1954, 1960, 1967–69; Indonesia 1958; Cuba 1959–61; Congo 1964; Peru 1965; Vietnam 1961–73; Laos 1964–73; Cambodia 1969–70; Grenada 1983; Lebanon 1983, 1984; Libya 1986; El Salvador mid-1980s; Nicaragua mid-1980s; Panama 1989; Iraq 1991–99; Kuwait 1991; Bosnia 1994, 1995; Sudan 1998; Afghanistan 1998; Yugoslavia 1999. Countries bombed "by accident" in 1998 and 1999 include Pakistan, Albania, Macedonia, and Bulgaria.

> William Blum, 'U.S. Serial Bombing: The Grim Record', *CovertAction Quarterly*, Number 67, Spring–Summer 1999.

❖

A crew member of the Enola Gay was able to say a few hours after dropping the bomb over Hiroshima, "I knew the Japs were in for it, but I felt no particular emotion about it."

John Whittier Treat, *Writing Ground Zero – Japanese Literature and the Atomic Bomb*, Chicago, University of Chicago, 1995, p. 17.

Treat quotes Col. William S. Parsons from *By the Bomb's Early Light*, by Paul Boyer.

❖

Its first practical application, at 8:15 on the morning of August 6, 1945, killed 300,000 people. It also killed the idea of the executioner. . . . Now we require nothing productive of our victims, but only the mathematical performance of their death – an instantaneous transformation from human being to useless residue – for audiences around the world.

> There was no boot-clad executioner, rather only a brilliant flash and, for some, a deafeningly loud noise. The degradation of human life in Auschwitz was still a perverse proof of human existence, if only because Nazi sadism required fellow human beings to submit to its display of power. There was no such proof in Hiroshima and Nagasaki. The intended audience was in Tokyo and Moscow, not the targets themselves. In the death camps individual human lives were rendered into pieces of common soap. Those lives, both as slave labor and then as material, made some ghastly reference to economic if not moral value. In Hiroshima and Nagasaki, however, individual lives were rendered into useless residue. Nothing "productive" was ever required of the victims.

John Whittier Treat, *Writing Ground Zero – Japanese Literature and the Atomic Bomb*, Chicago, University of Chicago, 1995, p. 15.

❖

We have manufactured death with such perfection that life feels counterfeit. The result that the exact moment when the act of atrocity begins now eludes us, as does its end, or its limit.

> It is easier to kill people either by means of gas chambers – or even more so, with high aerial atomic bombings – precisely because of this alienated relationship between victim and victimizer, indeed between any one victim and any other. The alienation commenced long ago,

perhaps as early as the guillotine ("that machine,"
as Foucault defines it, "for the production of
rapid and discreet deaths"); but by August 1945,
efficiency had increased exponentially along with
the capacity for depersonalization. . . . This is the
ultimate demoralized result of the process of
dehumanization now accepted as the tacit policy
of governments.

John Whittier Treat, *Writing Ground Zero — Japanese Literature and the Atomic Bomb*,
Chicago, University of Chicago, 1995, p. 16.

The atomic bomb was for its time the product of
the most advanced technology attained by the
species. Science, its ethos long privileged in
Western and Westernized cultures, and which
had been expected to aid in, if not actually bring
about, our liberation, became instead an abject
lesson in how our discoveries can be turned
against us. It is in this debilitating sense that
Hiroshima and Nagasaki hibikusha feel
themselves not simply the victims of war, but
even victims of the contradictions of
civilization itself.

John Whittier Treat, *Writing Ground Zero — Japanese Literature and the Atomic Bomb*,
Chicago, University of Chicago, 1995, p. 10.

❖

The sum and potential of human behavior presses on the imagination with a new
kind of darkness.

See George Steiner note above, in section 2.1.

❖

Like science and politics, our words have betrayed us: our languages, our silences,
complicit in our violent and complex poverty. . . . No matter how responsible, irresponsible, how personal, wise, or innocent, how clear or unintelligible our creations,
we feel they commune in devalued currencies and criminally suspect vocabularies.

No more words: language, its reliability already
devalued by philosophy, has become almost
criminally suspect in the wake of world wars.

It has even collaborated in our collective
victimhood. "Speaking always involves a
treason," noted Albert Camus, and Japanese
survivors of Camus' same war sometimes
arrived at the same conclusion as they attempt to
describe Hiroshima and Nagasaki. "What words
can we now use," mused writer Takenishi
Hiroko in an essay on the potential of
language after August 6th. "What words can we
now use, and to what ends? Even: what *are*
words?"

John Whittier Treat, *Writing Ground Zero — Japanese Literature and the Atomic Bomb*,
Chicago, University of Chicago, 1995, p. 27.

❖

Now we think of knowledge as that from which we must escape in order to create,
to find a place to call a beginning, and another place to call an end.

The experience of the atomic bomb, like a magnification of trauma in
general, presents the survivor with an eternal present, an endlessness, the telling of
which betrays not only the experience itself, but also those who did not survive.
Perhaps all memoirists of atrocious violence
experience such feelings of radical estrangement,
feelings that can so easily handicap writing; then
again, perhaps for all of us writing has to be, as
Barthes insisted, a "compromise between
freedom and remembrance."

John Whittier Treat, *Writing Ground Zero — Japanese Literature and the Atomic Bomb*,
Chicago, University of Chicago, 1995, p. 42.

See also Cathy Caruth, *Unclaimed Experience: Trauma, Narrative & History*, New York City,
Johns Hopkins, 1996.

❖

No matter how much we write, we are left with the feeling there is more to say.

Hiroshima poet Tokuno Koichi expresses doubts over whether literature can communicate the reality of August 6, 1945: "No matter how much one writes, one is left
with the feeling there is more to say."

John Whittier Treat, *Writing Ground Zero — Japanese Literature and the Atomic Bomb*,
Chicago, University of Chicago, 1995, p. 27.

❖

Consider the book ... full of uselessness ...

Merton quotes Ionesco as follows.

> The Universal and modern man is the man in a
> rush (i.e. a rhinoceros), a man who has no time,
> who is a prisoner of necessity, who cannot
> understand that *a thing might perhaps be without
> usefulness*; nor does he understand that, at
> bottom, it is the useful that may be a useless and
> back-breaking burden. If one does not
> understand the usefulness of the useless and
> the uselessness of the useful, one cannot understand
> art. And a country where art is not understood is
> a country of slaves and robots ...

Thomas Merton, 'Rain and the Rhinoceros', *Raids on the Unspeakable*, New York, New Directions, 1966, p. 21.

See also microlecture 2.3.

❖

... and accidents ...

> The lapse occurs frequently at breakfast and the
> cup dropped and overturned on the table is its
> well-known consequence.

Paul Virilio, *The Aesthetics of Disappearance*, trans. P. Beitchman, New York, Semiotext(e), 1991, p. 9.

See also almost anything else written by this author.

❖

... the book which places our distractions and our embarrassments center stage ...

See Richard Foreman note above, in section 2.1.

❖

... unfolds them like an artichoke, allows us to escape ourselves ...

> Think what it would be to have a work conceived
> from outside the *self*, a work that would let us

escape the limited perspective of the individual
ego, not only to enter into selves like our own
but to give speech to that which has no
language . . .

Italo Calvino, 'Multiplicity', *Six Memos for the Next Millennium*, Cambridge MA, Harvard, 1988, p. 124.

❖

Consider the necessary book of elevators . . .

See Rem Koolhaas note above, in section 2.1.

❖

. . . the book of strange invitations . . .

Put it together. It's a strange invitation.

Beck, 'Jack-Ass', *Odelay*, CD-24823, Los Angeles, Geffen, 1996.

❖

. . . about which we can say, "This book is not a book. It's not a song. Nor a poem. Nor thoughts."

This is not a book.
It's not a song.
Nor a poem. Nor thoughts.

Marguerite Duras, 'The Death of the Young British Pilot', *Writing*, trans. M. Polizzotti, Cambridge, Lumen, 1998, p. 49.

❖

I considered a book that might result from following some simple instructions: 1) fill your book with seeds; 2) cut holes in it; 3) hang it where there is wind.

Cut a hole in a bag filled with seeds of any kind
and place the bag where there is wind.

1961 Summer

Yoko Ono, 'Painting for the Wind', *Instruction Paintings*, New York, Weatherhill, 1995, p. 15.

❖ ❖ ❖

# 3. WHAT IS A FACT?

## 3.1 Thanksgiving-1: The impossible is a frog

We agreed that we would share a kind of impossible problem from which we would generate material individually, and then come together: a starting point.

> Lin Hixson, 'Soldier, Child, Tortured Man – The Making of a Performance', *Contact Quarterly*, Summer 1990.

❖

We unanimously elected Lin Hixson director.

Lin had ten years of directing experience in Los Angeles before the formation of Goat Island.

> Jacki Apple, 'The Life and Times of Lin Hixson: The LA Years', *The Drama Review*, Volume 35, Number 4 (T132), Winter 1991.

❖

> NO to spectacle no to virtuosity no to transformations . . .

> Yvonne Rainer, 'Some Retrospective Notes on a Dance for 10 People and 12 Mattresses Called *Parts of some Sextets*, Performed at the Wadsworth Atheneum, Hartford, Connecticut, and Judson Memorial Church, New York, March, 1965', postscript, in Mariellen Sandford (ed.) *Happenings and Other Acts*, New York, Routledge, 1995, p. 166.

❖

*Now I am a frog far away from the shadow of an idea.*

> Tatsumi Hijikata quoted by Mark Holborn, 'Tatsumi Hijikata and the Origins of Butoh', *Butoh – Dance of the Dark Soul*, New York, Aperture, 1985, p. 13.

❖

> Describe the last time you had sex.

> This starting point led to the creation of *We Got A Date*. See Carol Becker, 'Goat Island's *We Got A Date*', *Zones of Contention*, Albany, SUNY, 1996, and Stephen J. Bottoms, 'Re-staging Roy: Citizen Cohn and the Search for Xanadu', *Theatre Journal*, Vol. 48, No. 2, May 1996.

❖

Create an event of bliss/create an event of terror.

This starting point led to the creation of *Can't Take Johnny to the Funeral*. See Carol Becker, 'From Tantrums to Prayer: Goat Island's *Can't Take Johnny to the Funeral*', *Zones of Contention*, Albany, SUNY, 1996.

❖

Why were you in pain in such a beautiful place?

This starting point led to the creation of *It's Shifting, Hank*. See Goat Island, *Hankbook — Process and Performance of It's Shifting, Hank*, Chicago, Goat Island, 1994.

❖

Create a shivering homage.
Invent an arrival.
How do you say goodbye?

These three starting points led to the creation of *How Dear to Me the Hour When Daylight Dies*. See Stephen J. Bottoms, 'The Tangled Flora of Goat Island: Rhizome, Repetition, Reality', *Theatre Journal*, Vol. 50, No. 4, December 1998, and Goat Island, 'Illusiontext', *Performance Research*, Vol. 1, No. 3, Autumn 1996.

❖

*I look for phrases that can be performed as a task.*

Lin Hixson, 'Generating Movement for Our New Performance', unpublished document in possession of author, 1996, p. 2.

❖

There are oceans of facts.

Alfred North Whitehead, *Modes of Thought*, New York, Macmillan, 1938, p. 18.

❖

**3.2 Facts**
*Example #1: devouring*

Hijikata:
*Early spring was the busy season on the farm . . .*

Tatsumi Hijikata, 'Kazedaruma', trans. Nippon Services Corp., *Butoh — Dance of the Dark Soul*, New York, Aperture, 1985, p. 125.

❖

Karen lost a great deal of weight suddenly.

> Goat Island and the Students of the Sunflower Community School, Chicago, 'The Incredible Shrinking Man Essay & Board Game', *The Drama Review*, Vol. 43, No. 1, (T161), Spring 1999, especially 'The Incredible Shrinking, section 5.5: Mike Walker, Amelia Earhart, Scott Carey', by Karen Christopher.

❖

Mike Walker:
*I was like you once . . .*

> This speech rewrites the testimony of Mike Walker, transcribed from a recording made by Christian Farms, date unknown. It omits the anti-drug Gospel message of the original.

❖

One might find one's autobiography in the biography of another – the trope of a factual life, performed by a stand-in.

> See note on Ron Vawter and the stand-in above, in section 1.

❖

*Taking into your own body the idea that your wrist is not your own . . .*

> Tatsumi Hijikata, 'Kazedaruma', trans. Nippon Services Corp., *Butoh – Dance of the Dark Soul*, New York, Aperture, 1985, p. 126.

❖

The question is: Do they mean it when they say No Trespassing?

> John Cage, 'Where Are We Going? And What Are We Doing?', *Silence*, Hanover, NH, Wesleyan University Press, 1961, p. 197.

❖

*Example #2: collapsing*
We see ourselves as process immersed in process beyond ourselves. . . . This grasp of factuality is one extreme of thought. Namely, it is the concept of mere agitation of things agitated.

> Let us set these two topics of matter-of-
> fact and of importance in another light.

The notion of mere matter-of-fact is the
emergence into thought of the habit of mere
existence to coordinate itself with the necessities
of external activity. It is the recognition of the
goings-on of nature in which we, and all things
of all types, are immersed. It has its origin in the
thought of ourselves as process immersed in
process beyond ourselves. This grasp of
factuality is one extreme of thought. Namely, it is
the concept of mere agitation of things agitated.

Alfred North Whitehead, *Modes of Thought*, New York, Macmillan, 1938, p. 8.

❖

We break the rules, even our own rules. And how do we do that? By leaving plenty
of room for X quantities.

John Cage, 'Where Are We Going? And What Are We Doing?', *Silence*, Hanover,
NH, Wesleyan University Press, 1961, p. 197.

❖

Timothy McCain: *When we first work on a piece* . . .

Irene Tsatsos, 'Talking with Goat Island: An Interview with Joan Dickinson, Karen
Christopher, Matthew Goulish, Greg McCain and Tim McCain', *The Drama Review*,
Vol. 35, No. 4 (T132), Winter 1991, p. 71.

❖

Tim repeatedly watched the television footage of then-President George Bush . . .

Matthew Goulish, 'Process Text in 22 Parts', *Hankbook — Process and Performance of It's
Shifting, Hank*, Chicago, Goat Island, 1994, pp. 20–1.

❖

Process is the immanence of the infinite in the finite.

Process is the immanence of the infinite in the finite; whereby all bounds are burst,
and all inconsistencies dissolved.

Alfred North Whitehead, *Modes of Thought*, New York, Macmillan, 1938, p. 54.

❖

There is no reason to hold that confusion is less fundamental than is order.

> There is no reason to hold that confusion is less
> fundamental than is order. Our task is to evolve a
> general concept which allows room for both . . .

Alfred North Whitehead, *Modes of Thought*, New York, Macmillan, 1938, p. 50.

❖

*interruption: first words, not last words*

As will quickly become apparent to the reader, this book is an exploration, a first word, not a last word, an attempt to capture ideas.

> As will quickly become apparent to the reader,
> this study is a preliminary exploration, a first
> word, not a last word, an attempt to capture ideas
> and to suggest how they might be developed and
> tested.

Kevin Lynch, *The Image of the City*, Cambridge, MIT, 1960, p. 3.

❖

The convention of sincerity discourages me.

Chantal Akerman, *Directed by Chantal Akerman*, 1997.

❖

I write because of the good fortune I have to get mixed up in everything.

> I write because of the good fortune I have to get
> mixed up in everything, with everything; the
> good fortune to be in this battlefield, in this
> theater devoid of war, in the enlargement of this
> reflection.

Marguerite Duras, 'The Death of the Young British Pilot', *Writing*, trans. M. Polizzotti, Cambridge, Lumen, 1998, p. 55.

❖

*Example #3: haunting*

I found a photograph of a kabuki actor in the book *Childhood Years* by Jun'ichiro Tanizaki ...

Jun'ichiro Tanizaki, *Childhood Years*, trans. P. McCarthy, New York, Kodansha, 1989, p. 103.

❖

*Last Christmas I went back to visit our home farm.*

Bryan Saner, 'Plow and Anchor' from Goat Island, 'Notes on How Dear to Me the Hour When Daylight Dies', publication in possession of the author, 1996.

❖

Hijikata:
*We should take good care of our deceased. We've got to bring our dead close to us and lead our lives with them. The dead are my teachers.*

> ... the dead are my teachers. We should take good care of our deceased. Sooner or later, we too will be summoned. That's why we've got to learn these dreadful lessons while we're still alive; that's how we can keep our wits about us when the time comes. We've got to bring the dead close to us and lead our lives with them. There's nothing but brightness now. But I wonder if this brightness didn't arrive on the back of the darkness within us.

Tatsumi Hijikata, 'Kazedaruma', trans. Nippon Services Corp., *Butoh – Dance of the Dark Soul*, New York, Aperture, 1985, p. 127.

❖

No fact is merely itself.

Alfred North Whitehead, *Modes of Thought*, New York, Macmillan, 1938, p. 9.

❖

The earth rotates, and we move with it.

> The earth rotates; and we move with it, experiencing the routine of day and night as a prime necessity in our lives.

Alfred North Whitehead, *Modes of Thought*, New York, Macmillan, 1938, p. 7.

❖

### 3.3 The meeting place

I derived the opening paragraph on Srinivasa Ramanujan from the following sources.

> D. Crystal, ed., *The Cambridge Biographical Dictionary*, Cambridge, Cambridge University Press, 1996.

> George Gheverghese Joseph, *The Crest of the Peacock — Non-European Roots of Mathematics*, London, Penguin, 1990, pp. xi–xii, 293.

"What makes Ramanujan's work so seductive ... "

> Joseph quotes R. Kanigel, *The Man Who Knew Infinity: A Life of the Genius Ramanujan*, New York, Charles Scribner's Sons, 1991, pp. 349–50.

❖

It was said of Ramanujan that he considered each of the first hundred integers a personal friend.

> Alfred North Whitehead, *Modes of Thought*, New York, Macmillan, 1938, p. 47.

❖

... April 13, 1919 ... when the massacre of 379 unarmed civilians by troops under British command at Amritsar had devastated India.

> The killing of at least 379 unarmed people and the wounding of 2,000 more by troops under British command at Amritsar's Jallianwala Bagh occurred on 13 April 1919.

> Krishna Dutta and Andrew Robinson, *Rabindranath Tagore: The Myriad-Minded Man*, New York, St, Martin's Press, 1996, p. 215.

❖

Every example of friendship exhibits the particular characters of the friends.

> Alfred North Whitehead, *Modes of Thought*, New York, Macmillan, 1938, p. 58.

❖

In the full concrete connection of things, the characters of the things connected enter into the character of the connectivity which joins them.

> Alfred North Whitehead, *Modes of Thought*, New York, Macmillan, 1938, p. 58.

❖

Paragraph on GEOMETRY OF RAIN AND OF CLOUDS, including relation equation, extracted and abbreviated from Mandelbrot.

Benoit B. Mandelbrot, *The Fractal Geometry of Nature*, New York, W. H. Freeman and Co., 1983, p. 112.

❖

A partially understood pattern is more definite as to what it excludes than as to what its completion would include.

Alfred North Whitehead, *Modes of Thought*, New York, Macmillan, 1938, p. 52

❖

Understanding has two modes of advance, the gathering of detail within assigned pattern, and the discovery of a new pattern with its emphasis on new detail.

Thus understanding has two modes of advance,
the gathering of detail within assigned pattern,
and the discovery of novel pattern with its
emphasis on novel detail.

Alfred North Whitehead, *Modes of Thought*, New York, Macmillan, 1938, pp. 57–8.

❖

. . . we proposed structuring that material palindromically, to reflect the formula of pilgrimage, a self-reversing journey.

Victor Turner and Edith Turner, *Image and Pilgrimage in Christian Culture*, New York, Columbia University, 1978.

See especially Chapter One – Introduction: Pilgrimage as a Liminoid Phenomenon, pp. 1–39.

❖

As always we needed to break our own rules, to leave space for X quantities, to invite the audience inside.

See John Cage note in section 3.2 Facts, example #2 collapsing, above.

❖

In her essay, she wrote: never simplify the complex, or complicate the simple.

To love. To be loved. To never forget your own
insignificance. To never get used to the
unspeakable violence and the vulgar disparity of

life around you. To seek joy in the saddest
places. To pursue beauty to its lair. To never
simplify what is complicated or complicate what
is simple. To respect strength, never power.
Above all, to watch. To try to understand. To
never look away. And never, never to forget.

Arundhati Roy, 'The End of Imagination', *The Cost of Living*, New York, Random
House, 1999.

❖

Yet, there are no simple concepts, and upon examination, the notion of simplicity
itself becomes complicated.

There are no simple concepts. Every concept has
components and is defined by them. It therefore
has a combination. It is a multiplicity . . .

Gilles Deleuze and Felix Guattari, *What is Philosophy?*, trans. H. Tomlinson and G.
Burchell, New York, Columbia University, 1994, p. 15.

❖

Maybe when we began our little performance company, we thought a perfect performance could dismantle a bomb.

The video's narrator speaks of Ron Vawter, in advanced stages of AIDS-related illness,
performing Philoktotes in Brussels.

He wanted the play to be perfect, because if it
was perfect it might cure him.

Leslie Thornton, 'The Last Time I Saw Ron', video, 1994.

❖

Escape from ourselves, from the limited perspective of the individual ego.

See Italo Calvino note in section 2.2 above, 'Multiplicity', *Six Memos for the Next
Millennium*, Cambridge MA, Harvard, 1988, p. 124.

❖

Since each of us was several, there was already quite a crowd.

> The two of us wrote *Anti-Oedipus* together. Since each of us was several, there was already quite a crowd. Here we have made use of everything that came within range, what was closest as well as farthest away. We have assigned clever pseudonyms to prevent recognition. Why have we kept our own names? Out of habit, purely out of habit. To make ourselves unrecognizable in turn. To render imperceptible, not ourselves, but what makes us act, feel, and think. Also because it's nice to talk like everybody else, to say the sun rises, when everybody knows it's only a manner of speaking. To reach, not the point where one no longer says I, but the point where it is no longer of any importance whether one says I. We are no longer ourselves. Each will know his own. We have been aided, inspired, multiplied.

Gilles Deleuze and Felix Guattari, *A Thousand Plateaus — Capitalism and Schizophrenia*, trans. Brian Massumi, Minneapolis, University of Minnesota Press, 1987, p. 3.

❖

Our starting points, questions, structures and arrangements allowed our crowdness to exist in concert, to make a micro-universe.

Gilles Deleuze, *The Fold — Leibniz and the Baroque*, trans. Tom Conley, Minneapolis, University of Minnesota Press, 1993. See passage starting on p. 132 on *concertation*, the second aspect of harmony in Baroque music. (The first aspect is *spontaneity*.)

❖

Hijikata:
*I once actually took the water dipper from the kitchen sink . . .*

Tatsumi Hijikata, 'Kazedaruma', trans. Nippon Services Corp., *Butoh — Dance of the Dark Soul*, New York, Aperture, 1985, pp. 125–6.

❖

... a meeting place where facts, numbers, the complex and the simple, and the possibility of escape might coexist as friends.

The concept of the meeting place derives from Lin Hixson's brief introduction to Goat Island delivered at the Centre for Contemporary Arts, Glasgow, March 23, 1996.

> I like to think of Goat Island as a meeting place
> where these six people come together from
> different backgrounds and work together
> collaboratively to create performance works and
> make documents ...

Her use of the idea and the term in turn derived from Robert Bly's introduction to the poetry of Tomas Tranströmer.

> Tranströmer values his poems not so much as
> artifacts but as meeting places. Images from
> widely separated worlds meet in his poems. He
> said (in the letter to the Hungarian poets), "My
> poems are meeting places ... What looks at first
> like a confrontation turns out to be connection."

Tomas Tranströmer, *Truth Barriers*, trans. Robert Bly, San Francisco, Sierra Club, 1980, p. 5.

❖

Some words speak of events. Other words, events make us speak.

> ... Barthes ... subtly understands that language
> "is both boundary and perspective." He
> acknowledges that language, like Marx's
> "history," is something over which we are
> capable of exercising will, even if the conditions
> in which we do so are not of our own making.
> Perhaps the same point is made, with even more
> subtle an understanding, by Takenishi Hiroko in
> those lines that stand as an epigraph to this
> chapter: "There are words that speak of a ruined
> Hiroshima. And there are words that a ruined
> Hiroshima makes us speak."

John Whittier Treat, *Writing Ground Zero — Japanese Literature and the Atomic Bomb*, Chicago, University of Chicago, 1995, p. 31.

❖ ❖ ❖

# 4. WHAT IS AN INTRODUCTION?

## 4.1 X and questions (introduction to the introduction)

By the time I was 37 years old, I had coincidentally compiled 37 microlectures.

I derive the idea of a book's size reflecting the length of the author's life from Lyn Hejinian's, *My Life*, a book which she published at age 37, having constructed it as a work in 37 sections, with 37 sentences comprising each section. For the second edition, published eight years later, she added 8 sections (with 45 sentences comprising each section), and 8 sentences to each previous section, to account for her current age.

Lyn Hejinian, *My Life*, Los Angeles, Sun & Moon, 1987.

❖

My newfound editor . . .

Thanks to Talia Rodgers for her dialogue, support, and belief.

❖

I did not think the writing was really about performance. It wasn't *about* anything. Concerning aboutness . . .

> No sustained investigation of the painting can hope to reach summarizable conclusions. The painting's "aboutness" can be made manifest, but only as the tacit dimension of an inquiry that keeps producing what Blake calls "particular knowledge."

This briefly-rendered discourse derives from Edward Snow's study of Bruegel's 'Children's Games', *Inside Bruegel: the play of images in children's games*, New York, North Point Press, 1997, especially the above passage from p. 6.

❖

I thought of a young film director I had met in college . . .

This passage, including the parable of X, refers to Sam Raimi, who went on to direct *Evil Dead parts 1 & 2*, *Darkman*, *The Quick and the Dead*, *A Simple Plan*, and of course, his biggest hit to this day, the television show *Xena, Warrior Princess*.

❖

Question #3: What is a book?
Answer #3: A book is the night.

The repeated phrase, "A book is the night", derives from Marguerite Duras's statement, "An open book is also night." (See microlecture 4.1, The first chapter, and note to section 2.1 above). I shortened it from "an open book" to "a book", removed "also" and added "the" primarily for reasons of rhythm. In doing so, I sacrificed the accuracy of "an open book." Sometimes the reader comes to the realization that all the printed words make up only half of the book. Silence makes up the other half. This realization may come at night, when the book has been opened, and one perceives the expansiveness of the world. One must have the book open to receive this perception, since it relates to the sense of being inside the book – of the book, lying open, encompassing the world. I interpret her statement roughly this way, and although I abbreviate it and repeat it as a kind of building block in the Introduction, I do not intend to diminish the startling precision and sadness of the original.

❖

### 4.2 A method: a worm (conclusion to the introduction)
This was no doubt because my second source was Washington Irving's Rip Van Winkle.

> Washington Irving, *The Complete Tales of Washington Irving*, New York, Da Capo, 1998.

❖

As Calvino said, "Today I will begin by copying . . . "

> Today I will begin by copying the first sentences
> of a famous novel, to see if the charge of energy
> contained in that start is communicated to my
> hand, which, once it has received the right push,
> should run on its own.

> Italo Calvino, *If on a winter's night a traveler*, trans. William Weaver, New York, Harcourt Brace Jovanovich, 1981, p. 177.

❖

### 4.3 Thanksgiving-2: An introduction is a book from the outside

When one sees a car about to run down a child, one pulls the child onto the sidewalk.

> I derived this paragraph from the Willett, Manheim and Fried translation of Bertolt Brecht's poem 'The World's One Hope'. Carolyn Forché, ed., *Against Forgetting: Twentieth Century Poetry of Witness*, New York, W. W. Norton & Company, 1993, p. 219.

❖

How strange we are in the world, and how presumptuous our doings. . . . Only one response can maintain us: gratefulness.

> Abraham Joshua Heschel, 'Gratefulness', *I Asked for Wonder*, S. H. Dresner, ed., New York, Crossroad, 1996, p. 22.

❖

We feel helpless and incongruous, each with our tiny candle in the mist.

> Helpless and incongruous is man with all his
> craving, with his tiny candles in the mist.

> Abraham Joshua Heschel, 'Beyond Good Intentions', *I Asked for Wonder*, S. H. Dresner, ed., New York, Crossroad, 1996, p. 45.

❖

Is not all thought, as Heidegger pointed out, a form of thanksgiving?

> . . . and would have wept over this but instead
> thought back with thanksgiving (and was not all
> thought, as Heidegger pointed out, a form of
> thanksgiving?) to his professor at Morehouse,
> Benjamin Mays, who impressed upon him the
> importance of learning Henley's poem "Invictus"
> (It matters not how straight the gate . . . ).

> Charles Johnson, *Dreamer*, New York, Simon & Schuster, 1998, p. 17.

❖

## THANK YOU TO MY TEACHERS
(in reverse chronology)

Murray Mednick, John O'Keefe, and Maria Irene Fornes at Padua Hills; Dr Spencer, Conrad Hilberry, and Nelda Balch at Kalamazoo College; Stuart Dybek, who impressed upon me Calvino's significance one evening as we rode an elevator; Keith Spaulding, Jerry Hennessy, Connie and Eric Swanson at Frankenmuth High School and Middle School; Mr Snow, 4th grade math, and Miss Dearing, 3rd grade, at Harrington; Mrs Lameika, Cascades kindergarten; my grandparents, parents, my brother and his family; Mr Thackery, also known as Sir, the greatest fictional teacher. Now that I have become a teacher, I have begun to learn from my students.

❖

## VALUED COLLEAGUES AND FRIENDS

Carol Becker, Peggy Phelan, Smokey Hormel, Jack Murchie, Douglas Humble and Kristin Bonkemeyer, Ken Thompson, Steve Bottoms, Adrian Heathfield, Ross Birrell, Mark Waddell, Diana Warden, Forced Entertainment, Performance Research Journal, Charles Garoian, Henry Sayre, the teachers at Dartington College of Arts, the MFA Writing Program and the Liberal Arts Department of the School of the Art Institute of Chicago.

❖

I owe a debt which can never be repaid...

Peggy Phelan, *Mourning Sex – Performing Public Memories*, London, Routledge, 1997, p. x.

The accounts can never be balanced.

❖

... everyone who is now or has ever been a member of Goat Island performance group ...

1986–88: Matthew Goulish, Lin Hixson (director), Greg McCain, Timothy McCain
1988–89: Joan Dickinson, Matthew Goulish, Lin Hixson (director), Greg McCain, Timothy McCain
1990: Karen Christopher, Joan Dickinson, Matthew Goulish, Lin Hixson (director), Greg McCain, Timothy McCain
1991: Lydia Charaf, Karen Christopher, Matthew Goulish, Lin Hixson (director), Greg McCain, Timothy McCain
1991–95: Karen Christopher, Matthew Goulish, Lin Hixson (director), Greg McCain, Timothy McCain

1995–96: Karen Christopher, Matthew Goulish, Lin Hixson (director), Antonio Poppe, Bryan Saner

1997–2000: Karen Christopher, Matthew Goulish, Lin Hixson (director), Mark Jeffery, Bryan Saner

Adrian Blundell oversaw videography projects from 1994 to 1997; Dolores Wilber oversaw design projects in 1994 and 1995; Chantal Zakari oversaw design projects from 1995 to 1999. Lauren Martens has served as board member since 1991. C.J. Mitchell became company manager in 1998.

❖

People have asked me for my definition of music. This is it. It is work.

> People frequently ask me what my definition of
> music is. This is it. It is work. That is my
> conclusion.

John Cage, 'The Future of Music', *Empty Words*, Middleton, CT, Wesleyan University Press, 1979, p. 186.

❖

Rabbi Mendel's hasidim asked him why he did not write a book.

Martin Buber, 'Why Write a Book?', *Tales of the Hasidim – The Later Masters*, New York, Schocken, 1948, p. 288.

❖

Somewhere in a laboratory a perfect sheet of glass has been shattered . . .

Tim Hawkinson's wall sculpture 'Shatter' (1998) inspired this line. The piece uses a polyester sheet and aluminum tape to replicate an 84″ × 84″ shattered pane of glass.

❖

Can there be joy and laughter when always the world is ablaze?

> Can there be joy and laughter
> When always the world is ablaze?
> Enshrouded in darkness
> Should you not seek a light?

'Old Age', *The Dhammapada – The Path of Truth*, trans. The Venerable Balangoda Ananda Maitreya, Berkeley, Parallax, 1995, p. 41.

❖

A stranger asked a monk why he sat in front of a tree.

I have encountered two master teachers of Buddhism: Thich Nhat Hanh (Words can travel thousands of miles. Words can dismantle bombs), and the Venerable Samu Sunim, who told the story of the monk sitting in front of the tree.

❖

### 4.4  On proximity
*Hagioscope*
Hole made in a wall or pillar between an aisle and the chancel so that the main altar can be seen through it. Also known as a squint.

*Lepers' window*
Low side window on the south side of the chancel. It was so named from the belief that lepers, who could not enter the church, used it to see the mass in progress. The position of most such windows proves this to be untrue.

> Mark Child, *Discovering Church Architecture — A Glossary of Terms*, Princes Risborough, Shire Publications, 1976.

❖ ❖ ❖

## 5.  TO THE LISTENER

I have tried to compose some of your most particular experiences. . . . I realize that you are not a typical, but very particular, listener. . . . I realize that I have imagined you. Nevertheless, you have one invaluable advantage; you are the one listener about whom I really know something. . . . You are absolutely necessary for me – since it would be impossible for me to imagine this process other than in conjunction with a constantly imagined percipient. In this way creation and perception intermingle and are elements of the same complex phenomenon.

> I never try to lose sight of my basic aim – which is to compose the particular aesthetic experiences of my listener . . . I am perfectly well aware that my imagined listener is no typical listener, and that he is even probably very particular. For my work, however, he has one invaluable advantage: he is the one listener about whom I really know something. As such he is an element absolutely necessary for me in composing music – since it

would be impossible for me to imagine this
process without a constantly imagined percipient
of the work. In this way creation and perception
intermingle and are elements of the same complex
phenomenon.

Witold Lutoslawski, 'The Composer and the Listener', from Bernard Jacobson,
*A Polish Renaissance*, (20th Century Composers Series), London, Phaidon, 1996,
p. 67.

❖

You have begun to listen in such a way that you attend only to the note being
played at the moment – you try to forget a sound as soon as it stops and not to
anticipate what will happen next. Your concentration lapses frequently. . . . You have
a sense that almost anything can happen next: across boundaries, with many
connecting threads.

> Even though I had studied their history at length
> and knew what to expect, I was somewhat
> bewildered when I first heard them. In searching
> for a way to grasp the *Freeman Etudes*, I recalled
> the task of the violinist: to make sudden and
> dramatic changes from one note to the next. In
> these pieces, perhaps more than any other work by
> John Cage, there is a sense that anything can
> happen next: there are no boundaries, no
> connecting thread. Realizing that every note is
> completely separate from every other note, I have
> begun to try to listen in such a way that I attend
> only to the note being played at the moment – I
> try to forget a sound as soon as it stops and not
> to anticipate what will happen next. I lapse in my
> concentration rather frequently . . .

John Cage, *Freeman Etudes, Books One and Two*, New York, CD 32, Mode, 1993, from
notes by James Pritchett.

❖

You are not a thorough listener, and proud of it.

> I'm not
> a thorough
> listener

       & I'm
       proud
       of it

Eileen Myles, '1993', *School of Fish*, Santa Rosa, Black Sparrow, 1997, pp. 99–100.

❖

**You are the one I feel closest to, even if I do not know you personally.**

> I am not working to get many "fans" for myself;
> I do not want to convince, I want to find. I
> would like to find people who in the depths of
> their souls feel the same way as I do. That can
> only be achieved through the greatest artistic
> sincerity in every detail of music, from the
> minutest technical aspect to the most secret
> depths. I know that this standpoint deprives me
> of many potential listeners, but those who remain
> mean an immeasurable treasure for me. They are
> the people who are closest to me, even if I do not
> know them personally.

Bernard Jacobson, *A Polish Renaissance*, (20th Century Composers Series), London, Phaidon, 1996, p. 100, quoting Witold Lutoslawski.

❖

**. . . the limits of the next ten minutes . . .**

> Where in life we do everything we can to avoid
> anxiety, in art we must pursue it. This is
> difficult. Everything in our life and culture,
> regardless of our background, is dragging us
> away. Still, there is this sense of something
> imminent. And what is imminent, we find, is
> neither the past nor the future, but simply – the
> next ten minutes. The next ten minutes . . . We
> can go no further than that, and we need go no
> further.

Morton Feldman, 'The Anxiety of Art', in Thomas DeLio, *The Music of Morton Feldman*, New York, Excelsior Music Publishing Company, 1996, pp. 211–12.

❖

... the limits of bodies, the memory of bodies, and the motion we make toward and away from our own death ...

> [Caravaggio's] dramatic staging of the proof of Christ's resurrection is a proof that bring us, at once, too close to life and too close to death. If this scene [The Incredulity of St Thomas] of penetration is on the side of life, it is equally on the side of death. The painting's movement toward and away from the center of the hole mimics the motion we make toward and away from our own deaths.

Peggy Phelan, *Mourning Sex – Performing Public Memories*, London, Routledge, 1997, p. 35.

❖

the limits of blankness ...

> Blankness is an important quality that is completely ignored, especially by architects. It creates a kind of horror at its emptiness, but it is a very important thing to allow and to come to terms with. Our profession is indoctrinated to never allow something to remain empty, or undecided, or undetermined. That goes from the large scale to the small scale. Now there is an enormous rebirth of detailing. On one hand that is fantastic, but on the other hand it creates an incredible feeling of pressure: every chair has a hundred thousand ideas, an ambition to express something, perhaps the way it is put together, that simply draws attention to itself. Great attention is given to the packaging of space, but no attention to the space itself.

Rem Koolhaas, 'Seminar 1/21/91', *Conversations with Students*, New York, Princeton, 1996, p. 63.

❖

... the fractal scaling of cloudshapes, leaf veins, the circulatory system, heartbeats, the rhythms of sleep and insomnia ...

Benoit B. Mandelbrot, *The Fractal Geometry of Nature*, New York, W. H. Freeman and Co., 1983.

For more on the mathematical complexity of heartbeats and sleep, see the passages on "the dynamical heart" from the Inner Rhythms chapter of James Gleick, *Chaos: Making A New Science*, New York, Penguin, 1987, and Tim Etchells, 'Repeat Forever: Body, Death, Performance, Fiction', *Certain Fragments: Contemporary Performance and Forced Entertainment*, London, Routledge, 1999.

❖

We proceed in almost any direction, across boundaries, with many connecting threads.

See James Pritchett note above in this section.

❖

We proceed like the mosquito that bites the iron ox.

> When Master Yüeh-shan first visited Shih-t'ou, he asked, "I have studied the three vehicles and the twelve divisions of the teachings somewhat, but I have heard that in the south of China they point directly to men's minds in order to see the nature and achieve Buddhahood. Since I am still confused about this matter, I beg the master to give me some instructions."
>
> Shih-t'ou said, "This way you cannot get it, but that way you cannot get it either. Whether it is this way or not, you cannot get it." As Yüeh-shan did not understand, Shih-t'ou said, "Go to Kiangsi and ask Great Master Ma-tsu."
>
> Yüeh-shan took his advice and went to Ma-tsu's place, where he asked the same question. Ma-tsu said, "Sometimes I teach people by raising my eyebrows and twinkling my eyes. At other times I do not teach people by raising my eyebrows or twinkling my eyes. The times when I raise my eyebrows and twinkle my eyes is correct; the time when I do not raise my eyebrows or twinkle my eyes is incorrect."

> Under the influence of these words,
> Yüeh-shan had a great awakening; but, having
> nothing with which to show his gratitude, he
> merely lowered his head and bowed.
>     Ma-tsu asked, "What truth have you seen
> that makes you bow?"
>     Yüeh-shan said, "When I was at Shih-
> t'ou's place I was like a mosquito biting the back
> of an iron ox."
>     Ma-tsu sanctioned it.

Robert E. Buswell, Jr., *Tracing Back the Radiance: Chinul's Korean Way of Zen*, Honolulu, Kuroda Institute/University of Hawaii, 1991, p. 183.

❖

We proceed with no need to fear or to hope, but only to find new ways of under-standing.

> There is no need to fear or to hope, but only to
> look for new weapons.

Gilles Deleuze, 'Postscript on the Societies of Control' in Neal Leach, ed., *Rethinking Architecture*, New York, Routledge, 1997, p. 309.

Given the devotion to nonviolence evident in this introduction, I decided to alter the last word of Deleuze's sentence. The reader may consider this a gesture of intellectual disarmament: not weapons, but understanding; or simply a matter of preference for a more peaceful language. "The question is not one of good or bad but of specificity." See Deleuze and Guattari's 'Treatise on Nomadology', p. 390, *A Thousand Plateaus*, and also Fredric Jameson, 'Marxism and Dualism in Deleuze', *The South Atlantic Quarterly* 96:3, Duke University Press, Summer 1997.

❖ ❖ ❖

## 0.  WHAT IS A MICROLECTURE?

❖

### First book: bookmark (1969)
(*One fish, two fish, red fish, blue fish*)

Dr Seuss, *One fish, two fish, red fish, blue fish*, New York, Beginner Books, Distributed by Random House, 1960.

### Microlude (January, 1996)
We see in Kurtág's way of thinking . . .

> Kurtág, Lutoslawski, Gubaidulina, Arditti String Quartet edition 9 MO 789007, 1994, (includes Hommage to Mihály András − 12 microludes), notes by Hartmut Lück.

❖

### The golden boat (April 13, 1996)
Finally, speaking here at Dartington gives me the opportunity to evoke the spirit of the Bengali writer Rabindranath Tagore, whose educational innovations in India in the first half of the twentieth century inspired the founders of this institution.

> On Tagore's relationship to Dartington, see Krishna Dutta and Andrew Robinson, *Rabindranath Tagore: The Myriad-Minded Man*, New York, St, Martin's Press, 1996, p. 292.

❖

In his poem "The Golden Boat" Tagore tells the story . . .

> Rabindranath Tagore, "The Golden Boat", *Selected Poems*, trans. William Radice, New York, Penguin, 1985, p. 53.

❖ ❖ ❖

## 1.   REPETITION
April 13, 1996, Performance Writing Symposium at Dartington College of Art.

❖ ❖

### 1.1   A misunderstanding
A few years ago, a producer whose name was Rollo . . .

My use of the name Rollo to connote a critically unimaginative individual derives from the writings of composer Charles Ives. Ives' written complaints about "naysayers" and "hidebound" critics, invariably rename them Rollo. In his second string quartet, Ives also named each of the four musical parts. The second violinist, who expresses the most traditional tunes, is named Rollo. He has the responsibility of maintaining "traditional" order among the aggressively heterogeneous parts. See Alan Rich, *American Pioneers: Ives to Cage and Beyond*, London, Phaidon, 1995, pp. 53–4.

Repetition is only repetition if . . .

> Or you may leave it forever and never return to it,
> for we possess nothing. Our poetry now is the
> realization that we possess nothing. Anything
> therefore is a delight (since we do not possess it)
> and thus need not fear its loss. We need not
> destroy the past: it is gone; at any moment, it
> might reappear and seem to be and be the
> present. Would it be a repetition? Only if we
> thought we owned it, but since we don't, it is
> free, and so are we.

John Cage, 'Lecture on Nothing', *Silence*, Hanover NH, Wesleyan University Press, 1961, p. 110.

❖

. . . the repetition of ideas of deliberate limitation.

> The concept of ritual in much of my music
> pertains mainly to the handling of short repetitive
> melodic and rhythmic ideas. This is not in any
> Minimalist sense, but in a continual isorhythmic
> interplay or by the juxtaposition of ideas of
> deliberate limitation, which either remain constant
> throughout or which gradually change through
> integral transformation.

James MacMillan, notes on 'Three Dawn Rituals', *Music of James MacMillan*, Catalyst, 09026 61916 2, 1993.

❖ ❖

**1.2   Learning to read**

Marguerite Duras, *Summer Rain*, trans. Barbara Bray, London, Macmillan, 1992, pp. 6, 7, 9, 10, 138.

❖ ❖

**1.4   Proliferation and suffering**

John Lechte, 'Gilles Deleuze', *Fifty Key Contemporary Thinkers, from structuralism to postmodernity*, London, Routledge, 1994, pp. 102–4.

❖

Masuji Ibuse, *Black Rain*, trans. John Bester, New York, Kodansha, 1979, pp. 255, 259.

❖ ❖

### 1.5   Multiplicity

Morton Feldman, *For Christian Wolff*, notes by Christian Wolff and Walter Zimmerman, Berlin, hat ART 3–61201/2, 1992.

❖

I have rewritten the story titled "The House of Weddings".

Martin Buber, *Tales of the Hasidim, The Later Masters*, New York, Schocken, 1948, p. 314.

❖ ❖ ❖

## 2 .   CRITICISM

July 22, 1996, Goat Island Summer School, Centre for Contemporary Arts, Glasgow.

❖ ❖

### 2.1   The example of glass

On the threshold of this landscape we might pause to recall the writer Isaac Babel who described his grandmother's sobering admonition when, as a child, he told her he wanted to grow up to be a writer, and she replied, "To be a writer, you must know everything."

> "Study," she says with force, "study, you will attain everything – wealth and fame. You must know everything. Everyone will fall down and abase themselves before you. Everyone must envy you. Don't have faith in human beings. Don't have friends. Don't lend them money. Don't lend them your heart."

Isaac Babel, 'Childhood. With Grandmother', *Collected Stories*, trans. David McDuff, New York, Penguin, 1994, p. 26.

❖ ❖

## 2.2  The example of windows

Kevin Volans, Notes to *Dancers on a Plane*, *5th String Quartet*, Collins Classics, 14172, 1995.

❖ ❖

## 2.3  The example of rain

Thomas Merton, 'Rain and the Rhinoceros,' *Raids on the Unspeakable*, New York, New Directions, 1966, pp. 9–23.

❖ ❖ ❖

## 3.  PEDAGOGY

November 15, 1996, Performance, Culture, Pedagogy Symposium, Penn State, Pennsylvania.

❖ ❖

## 3.1  The unlearnable

Alexandra David-Neel, *Initiations and Initiates in Tibet*, New York, Dover, 1993, pp. 40–1.

❖ ❖

## 3.2  Anthem

I extracted this microlecture from my travel journals. The Zagreb workshop was sponsored by the Eurokaz Festival, The Suitcase Fund, and Arts International. Goat Island members at the time included Lin Hixson, Karen Christopher, Bryan Saner, Antonio Poppe, Adrian Blundell, and myself.

❖ ❖

## 3.3  The Ceremony

Oxford English Dictionary on 'pedagogy'.

❖

"We may still pity, but it is hard for us to comprehend the true dimensions of other people's loss."

> Dubravka Ugrešić, 'The Confiscation of Memory', *The Culture of Lies*, trans. Celia Hawkesworth, University Park, PA, Pennsylvania State University Press, 1998, p. 226.

❖

As the Japanese novelist Kenzaburo Oe has pointed out . . .

> As a definition of Shiki's "compassion," I would propose something to the effect of "an active yet almost automatic ability to enter into the feelings of another person." This comes very close to "imagination," reminding me of what Rousseau says in *Emile* on the subject of education: that "only the imagination can teach us another's pain."

> Kenzaburo Oe, 'Compassion', *A Healing Family*, New York, Kodansha, 1995, p. 39.

❖

". . . we must always begin by asking questions . . . "

> Science is curiosity, discovering things and asking why. Why is it so? Indeed, science is the opposite of knowledge. Science asks the why and how questions and therefore is the process of questioning, not the acquisition of information. We must always begin by asking questions, not by giving answers. We must create interest in things, phenomena, processes.

> Victor F. Weisskopf, 'Teaching Science', *The Privilege of Being a Physicist*, New York, W. H. Freeman and Company, 1988, p. 31.

❖

"I think I am a cultural maximalist . . . "

> I'm a minimalist in the sense that I use as few notes as possible, but a maximalist in the cultural sense. I really do think that, say, Indian music is as impressive in its own right as the late Beethoven quartets. I see all music as

basically one. The world is getting smaller and
we suspect that the universe is teeming with life,
so what is going to happen when we confront all
those extraterrestrial musics?! That's not going
to have anything to do with European music or
world music.

Geoff Smith and Nicola Walker Smith, 'George Crumb,' *American Originals –
Interviews with 25 Contemporary Composers*, London, Faber & Faber, 1994, p. 101.

❖

With ceremonial regret ...

With ceremonial regret I lowered a seed
into the earth as though I laid it to its final
rest ...
If this seed live again then so shall I.
Which, of course, is sheer nonsense
placed in the service of a tongue too long in
the damp sleep of its mouth.

Russell Edson, 'The Ceremony', *The Tunnel: Selected Poems*, Oberlin OH, Oberlin
College Press, 1994, p. 174.

❖ ❖ ❖

## 4 . BEGINNINGS
December 6, 1996, N.A.M.E. Gallery Speakeasy, Chicago.

❖ ❖

### 4.1 The First Chapter
A book is the night.

Marguerite Duras, 'Writing', *Writing*, trans. M. Polizzotti, Cambridge, Lumen,
1998, p. 14.

See also note in Introduction, section 2.2.

❖

. . . like Joshua, who empowered by the word and by music halted the very sun in the sky . . .

> 'Sun, stand thou still at Gibeon,
> and thou Moon in the valley of Ai´jalon.'
> And the sun stood still, and the moon stayed . . .

Joshua 10:12–13, The Holy Bible, Revised Standard Version, New York, Thomas Nelson & Sons, 1953, p. 235.

❖

Bram Stoker, *Dracula*, New York, Bantam, 1981.

❖ ❖

## 4.2 The first line
The list of first lines derives from the following works.

Gabriel García Márquez, *One Hundred Years of Solitude*, trans. Gregory Rabassa, New York, Avon, 1971.

Jorge Luis Borges, commentary on 'The Dead Man', *The Aleph and Other Stories 1933–1969*, trans. Norman Thomas Di Giovanni and the author, New York, E. P. Dutton, 1978.

Fyodor Dostoyevsky, *Crime and Punishment*, trans. Constance Garnett, quoted in Italo Calvino, *If on a winter's night a traveller*, trans. William Weaver, New York, Harcourt Brace Jovanovich, 1981, pp. 177–8.

Franz Kafka, *Complete Stories*, 'The Metamorphosis', trans. Willa and Edwin Muir, New York, Schocken, 1976.

Flannery O'Conner, 'Everything That Rises Must Converge', *Everything That Rises Must Converge*, New York, Farrar, Straus and Giroux, 1970.

Sherwood Anderson, *Winesburg, Ohio*, New York, Random House, 1947.

Virginia Woolf, *The Waves*, New York, Harcourt Brace Jovanovich, 1978.

Herman Melville, *Moby-Dick*, New York, Penguin, 1972.

Rabindranath Tagore, *The Home and the World*, trans. Surendranath Tagore, New York, Penguin, 1985.

James Joyce, *Portrait of the Artist as a Young Man*, New York, Viking, 1969.

Samuel Beckett, *Malone Dies*, London, Calder, 1959.

Italo Calvino, *If on a winter's night a traveler*, trans. William Weaver, New York, Harcourt Brace Jovanovich, 1981.

❖

. . . you never imagined that your work was to discover your work, and then with all your heart to give yourself to it.

> Your work is to discover your work
> And then with all your heart
> To give yourself to it.

*Dhammapada — The Sayings of the Buddha*, 'Yourself', trans. Thomas Byrom, Boston, Shambhala, 1993, p. 45.

❖

Stuart Dybek, 'Pet Milk', *The Coast of Chicago*, New York, Knopf, 1990.

❖

Marconi, inventor of the telegraph, came to believe at the end of his life that once a sound has been generated it doesn't die, but simply grows fainter and fainter, and given a sensitive enough ear and the right place to listen, one could hear it forever.

> Because Marconi had this strange idea, it was
> the end of his life, that once a sound has been
> generated, it doesn't die, it simply gets fainter
> and fainter. And what he was trying to do was to
> get listening equipment sufficiently sensitive
> that he could pick up these distant, historic
> sounds.

Gavin Bryars, ' "Titanic" Final Hymn Given New Chords', *All Things Considered*, National Public Radio, April 14, 1995.

❖ ❖

## 4.3 The first beginning

Milic Capek, 'TIME', *Dictionary of the History of Ideas*, Philip P. Wiener, ed., New York, Charles Scribner's Sons, 1973, p. 389.

❖

Albert Camus, *The Myth of Sisyphus and other essays*, Justin O'Brien tr., New York, Vintage, Random House, 1955.

❖

The rebel is Sisyphus. The rock is peace.

> . . . as punishment for his human understanding,
> he was condemned to push a heavy boulder up
> the side of a hill for the rest of time. The name
> of this stone is peace.

Hans Magnus Enzensberger, *Civil Wars*, New York, The New Press, 1993, p. 71.

❖

Martin Buber, 'The First Page', *Tales of the Hasidim – The Early Masters*, New York, Schocken, 1947, p. 232.

❖ ❖ ❖

## 5. HAIR
January 6, 1997, contribution to *hairinquiry* website by Anne Wilson.

❖ ❖

### 5.1 Two invitations
Anne Wilson, *an inquiry about hair*,

> http://www.anu.edu.au/ITA/CSA/textiles/hairinquiry/, 1996.

❖

Everything we do, we do by invitation. The invitation comes either from oneself or from another person.

> Everything we do is done by invitation. That
> invitation comes either from oneself or from
> another person.

John Cage, 'On Having Received the Carl Sczuka Prize for Roaratorio', *Roaratorio*, 28/29, Kew Gardens NY, Mode Records CD, 1992.

❖

I have had my invitations to this world, and thus my life has been blessed.

> I have had my invitation to this world's festival,
> and thus my life has been blessed.

Rabindranath Tagore, verse 16, *Gitanjali* [Song offering], Boston, Branden Publishing Company, 1992.

### 5.2 *Our Cancer*
It felt more like a position, more like folding in upon myself.

> And when an organism dies, it does not really
> vanish, but folds in upon itself . . .

Gilles Deleuze, *The Fold – Leibniz and the Baroque*, trans. Tom Conley, Minneapolis, University of Minnesota Press, 1993, p. 8.

It is so embarrassing to live!

Abraham Joshua Heschel, 'Gratefulness', *I Asked for Wonder*, S. H. Dresner, ed., New York, Crossroad, 1996, p. 22.

I felt abandoned by everything. A great sorrow fell upon my soul. I walked across the fields without salvation. I pulled a branch from some unknown bush, broke it, and brought it to my upper lip. I understood immediately that all people are innocent. We walk thousands of years. We call the sky "sky" and the sea "sea." All things will change one day, and we too with them.

> XXVII:
> One day when I was feeling abandoned by
> everything and a great sorrow fell slowly on my
> soul, walking across the fields without salvation,
> I pulled a branch from some unknown bush.
> I broke it and brought it to my upper lip. I
> understood immediately that man is innocent.
>
> XXVIII:
> We walk thousands of years. We call the sky
> 'sky' and the sea 'sea.' All things will change
> one day and we too with them . . .

Odysseas Elytis, XXVII-XXVIII, *The Little Mariner*, trans. Olga Broumas, Port Townsend WA, Copper Canyon Press, 1988, pp. 120–1.

This paragraph later transformed into Bryan Saner's closing speech in the Goat Island performance *The Sea & Poison*.

❖ ❖

### 5.3  Learning how to leave the world

Marguerite Duras, *Hiroshima Mon Amour*, trans. Richard Seaver, New York, Grove, 1961, pp. 61–2.

❖

Russell Edson, 'A Man With a Tree on His Head, *The Tunnel: Selected Poems*, Oberlin OH, Oberlin College Press, 1994, p. 52.

❖

Martin Buber, 'Playing with a Watch' *Tales of the Hasidim — Later Masters*, New York, Schocken, 1948, p. 234.

❖

Yoko Ono, 'Painting To Hammer A Nail', *Instruction Paintings*, New York, Weatherhill, 1995, p. 31.

❖ ❖ ❖

## 6.  WOMEN AND DIRECTING
March 24, 1997, Women on Art Conference, Centre for Contemporary Arts, Glasgow.

❖ ❖

### 6.1  The Creature from the Black Lagoon
Zen Buddhism passage derived from:

Thich Nhat Hanh, 'No-Self', *Thundering Silence — Sutra on the Better Way to Catch a Snake*, Berkeley, Parallax Press, 1993, pp. 39–40.

❖ ❖

## 6.2 Everything about life

Maria Irene Fornes quote derived from:

Kathleen Betsko and Rachel Koenig, 'Maria Irene Fornes', *Interviews with Contemporary Women Playwrights*, New York, Beech Tree Books/Quill Edition, 1987, p. 156.

❖

"Do you really imagine you know everything about life?"

Albert Camus, *The Plague*, trans. S. Gilbert, New York, Vintage, 1991, p. 129.

❖ ❖

## 6.3 Slow thinking

Anita Finkel, 'Gunsmoke', *The New Dance Review*, Vol. IV, No. 2, pp. 4, 6.

❖

Kenzaburo Oe, *A Quiet Life*, trans. K. Yanagishita & W. Wetherall, New York, Grove, 1996, pp. 78–9.

❖

... composer Witold Lutoslawski's statement that the function of the first movement in his compositions is to make the audience impatient.

> I have thought a lot about large scale closed forms. I was not always happy with the Brahmsian tradition. In Brahms there are two main movements, the first and the fourth. In my experience as a listener, that is too much. Too much substance within [a short span of] time. I believe that the ideal relationship is achieved in Haydn's symphonies. And I thought that perhaps I could find some other way to achieve this balance. My solution is to view the first movement as preparation for the main movement. The first movement must engage, interest – it must intrigue. But it must not give complete satisfaction. It must make us hungry, and, finally, even impatient. That is the right moment to introduce the main movement. That is my solution, and I think it works rather well.

Steven Stucky, 'Comments: Witold Lutoslawski, Symphony No. 4', Chicago Symphony Orchestra Notebook, February 20–25, 1997, quoting Lutoslawski.

❖

Johannes Birringer, 'Pina Bausch: Dancing Across Borders', *Theatre, Theory, Postmodernism*, Bloomington and Indianapolis, Indiana University Press, 1991, p. 137.

❖ ❖

## 6.4  Beauty

John Cage, 'Lecture on Something', *Silence*, Hanover NH, Wesleyan University Press, 1961, p. 131.

❖

Elizabeth LeCompte, 'Brace Up!', *Felix*, Vol. I, No. 3, p. 58.

❖

Susan Letzler Cole, *Directors in Rehearsal*, New York, Routledge, 1992, p. 93 and note 5.

❖ ❖

## 6.5  Body through which the dream flows
. . . A young music student at a midwestern college . . .

I checked the accuracy of this story with George Crumb on March 25, 2000 at the Chicago Museum of Contemporary Art. He explained that the events, which occurred during a performance of *Eleven Echoes of Autumn*, did not take place at a midwestern college, and nothing was thrown at the stage. "At the end of it, you heard some boos. So I started booing too."

John Adams, notes to *Violin Concerto*, Nonesuch Records 79360–2, 1996.

❖ ❖ ❖

## 7. TECHNOLOGIES OF DYING
April 11, 1997, 3rd Annual Performance Studies Conference: Performance and Technology, Atlanta.

Peggy Phelan conceived the title 'Technologies of Dying' for our panel which also included Adrian Heathfield, and for which I wrote this microlecture series.

❖ ❖

## 7.1 What is a machine?

*Question #1: What is innocence?*

> Tadeusz Kantor, trans. M. Kobialka, 'Silent Night (Cricotage) 1990; III Imprints:
> Army', *A Journey Through Other Spaces – Essays and Manifestos, 1944–1990*, Berkeley/Los
> Angeles/London, University of California Press, 1993, pp. 189–90.

❖ ❖

## 7.2 What BECOMES a machine?

*Deterritorialization* is the movement . . . overlaid by *reterritorializations* on property, work,
and money.

> Gilles Deleuze and Felix Guattari, trans. Brian Massumi, *A Thousand Plateaus –*
> *Capitalism and Schizophrenia*, Minneapolis, University of Minnesota Press, 1987,
> p. 508.

❖

The belief in the moral force of the machine . . . as far preferable to himself.'

> Francis McKee, 'Deep Blue', manuscript essay loaned by the author, p. 7.

❖

. . . artists and architects saw in the machine an elegant freedom . . . their beauty
arrived without morality.

> This beauty discerned in the machine was seen
> as a freedom from the domination of the ancient
> classical forms. Machines, each one designed as
> a solution to a specific problem, derived their
> essential structures from the principles of
> engineering and science. Their beauty arrived
> without the age-old orthodoxies of form and the
> Platonic ideal.

> Francis McKee, 'Deep Blue', manuscript essay loaned by the author, p. 2.

❖

For contemporary theorist Bruno Latour, the machine is a transparent entity,
perpetually signalling the history of the human endeavor which ensured its existence.

> Francis McKee, 'Deep Blue', manuscript essay loaned by the author, p. 8.

> Bruno Latour, *Aramis, or The Love of Technology*, Cambridge, Harvard, 1996.

... to the most recent test cockroach outfitted with a microchip helmet ...

'Japan's latest advance: Robo-roach', Associated Press, January 10, 1997.

❖

... historians and scientists have identified a growing world of cyborgs, discerning a sharp intensification of the phenomenon as a result of the Second World War.

Francis McKee, 'Deep Blue', manuscript essay loaned by the author, pp. 4–5.

❖

The new forms resulting from this alignment ... 'The house is a machine for living in.'

Francis McKee, 'Deep Blue', manuscript essay loaned by the author, p. 2.

❖

The extract of J. R. Oppenheimer's speech derives from the NBC News archives, Washington. I transcribed and arranged this version from the sampling used by Jocelyn Pook in her composition, 'Oppenheimer', from *Deluge*, Virgin Records CDVE 933.

❖ ❖

### 7.3   Memory of a cloud
*Memory #1: cloud from the outside*
... the cloud in at least one instance had its explosive roar added by a modified phonograph with a potentiometer-controlled motor speed, playing a slowed down recording of a waterfall.

Ray Brunelle, 'The Art of Sound Effects, Part 2', *Experimental Musical Instruments*, Vol. 12, No. 2, December, 1996, p. 27.

❖

*Memory #2: cloud from the inside*
This paragraph derives from the following sources.

John Whittier Treat, *Writing Ground Zero — Japanese Literature and the Atomic Bomb*, Chicago, University of Chicago Press, 1995, pp. 10–11, note 37.

Takashi Nagai, *The Bells of Nagasaki*, trans. W. Johnston, New York, Kodansha, 1994, pp. 28, 41.

❖

*Memory #3: anthem of innocence*
Contemporary cultures produce myths about themselves . . . or the myth reality.

Dubravka Ugrešić, 'Yugo-Americana', *Have a Nice Day — From the Balkan War to the American Dream*, trans. Celia Hawkesworth, New York, Viking, 1995, p. 105.

❖

Jimmie Dodd, lyrics of 'Mickey Mouse March' from The Mickey Mouse Club, Walt Disney Music Company, 1955.

Additional Mickey Mouse Club research done at the Museum of Broadcast Communications, Chicago.

❖ ❖

**7.4   TOMORROWLAND**

Heinz Haber, *Our Friend the Atom*, Foreword by Walt Disney, New York, Walt Disney Publications, Simon & Schuster, 1956, pp. 10–11.

❖ ❖

**7.5   The Golem of Prague**
*Question #1: What is a machine?*

Primo Levi, 'The Scribe', *Other People's Trades*, trans. R. Rosenthal, New York, Summit Books, 1989, pp. 88–89.

❖

Jorge Luis Borges, with Margarita Guerrero, 'The Golem', *The Book of Imaginary Beings*, trans. N. T. di Giovanni, New York, E. P. Dutton, 1978, pp. 112–14.

❖

*Question #2: What is dying?*

Gustav Meyrink, *The Golem*, trans. E. F. Bleiler, New York, Dover, 1986, pp. 65–6.

❖

*Question #3: What is innocence?*
It is the ardent, eccentric, intense ... a new land, a universe.

> Finally, the earth is not the opposite of D: This
> can already be seen in the mystery of the
> "natal," in which the earth as ardent, eccentric,
> or intense focal point is outside the territory and
> exists only in the movement of D. More than
> that, the earth, the glacial, is Deterritorialization
> par excellence: that is why it belongs to the
> Cosmos, and presents itself as the material
> through which human beings tap cosmic forces.
> We could say that the earth, as deterritorialized,
> is itself the strict correlate of D. To the point
> that D can be called the creator of the earth –
> of a new land, a universe, not just a reterritorialization.

Gilles Deleuze and Felix Guattari, *A Thousand Plateaus – Capitalism and Schizophrenia*, trans. Brian Massumi, Minneapolis, University of Minnesota Press, 1987, p. 509.

❖

Mario Savio's famous speech was quoted in newspaper obituaries around the country on November 14, 1996.

See also Wendy Lesser, 'Speech With the Weight of Literature', *The New York Times Book Review*, November 17, 1996.

❖ ❖ ❖

## 8. HOW DOES A WORK WORK WHERE?

June 14, 1997, Visual Performance & Performance Writing Student Degree Show Forum, Dartington College of Arts, Dartington, England.

The students composed the question, which I took as a title for this microlecture series. The series derives its ideas, as well as some specific sentences and phrases, from only one work:

Gilles Deleuze, *The Fold – Leibniz and the Baroque*, trans. Tom Conley, Minneapolis, University of Minnesota Press, 1993.

❖ ❖

## 8.1   What is a work?

... anything which is noticeable must be made up of parts which are not ...

> For anything which is noticeable must be made
> up of parts which are not.

ibid. p. 60, n. 2.

❖

We feel momentarily overwhelmed, not just by the startling structures and figures, but also by the textures.

> Then matter has not only structures and figures
> but also *textures*, insofar as it comprises these
> masses of monads from which it cannot be
> detached.

ibid. p. 115.

❖

A work is an object overflowing its frame ...

> The object itself overflows its frame in order to
> enter into a cycle or series, and now the concept
> is what is found increasingly compressed,
> interiorized, wrapped in an instance that can
> ultimately be called "personal."

ibid. p. 125.

❖ ❖

## 8.2   What is work?

> **This man is free,**
> **not because he is determined from within,**
> **but because every time**
> **he constitutes the motive of the event that he produces.**

> The automaton is free not because it is
> determined from within, but because every time
> it constitutes the motive of the event that it
> produces.

ibid. p. 72.

❖

**What he does, he does entirely,
that being what comprises his liberty.**

If Adam were capable of not sinning, the
damned could free themselves: it would suffice
to have the soul take another amplitude, another
fold, or another inclination. It can be stated that
the soul cannot do so, except in another world,
one that is incompossible with ours. Yet clearly,
that it cannot do so signifies that the soul would
be other by doing so: what it does, it does
entirely, that being what comprises its liberty.

ibid. p. 71.

❖  ❖  ❖

## 9.  THE KALEIDOSCOPIC SELF

August 19, 1997, *P-Form Magazine*.

❖  ❖

### 9.1  What is a barbarian?
*Question #1: Who is excluded?*

The somewhat disputed etymology of *barbarian*, and the etymology of *nation*,
derive from the *Oxford English Dictionary*.

❖

*Question #2: Who is included?*

Etienne Balibar, 'The Nation Form: History and Ideology', *Race, Nation, Class —
Ambiguous Identities*, Balibar & Wallerstein, New York, Verso, 1988, p. 86, including
epigraph from Jacques Derrida's *Margins of Philosophy*.

❖

*Question #3: Who has no beard?*
Text derived from Case #4, and commentary to Case #7, of Mumonkan.

*Two Zen Classics — Mumonkan and Hekiganroku*, trans. with commentaries by Katsuki Sekida, New York, Weatherhill, 1996.

*The Shambhala Dictionary of Buddhism and Zen*, trans. M. Kohn, Boston, Shambhala, 1991.

❖ ❖

## 9.2   The stalwart words of Gibson's Wallace

Kirsty Scott, 'The fatal attraction', *The Herald* (Scottish newspaper), August 6, 1997.

Andrew McDonald (William Pierce), *The Turner Diaries*, New York, Barricade Books, Inc. 1996.

❖

Robert Siegel, 'Reformed Racist Spreads the Word About Tolerance', Floyd Cochran Interview, *All Things Considered*, National Public Radio, air date June 5, 1995.

❖

Racist organizations refuse to be designated as such . . . the organization of nationalism into individual political movements inevitably has racism underlying it.

Etienne Balibar, 'Racism and Nationalism', *Race, Nation, Class — Ambiguous Identities* Balibar & Wallerstein, New York, Verso, p. 37.

❖

John Lechte, 'Hannah Arendt', *Fifty Key Contemporary Thinkers — from structuralism to postmodernity*, London, Routledge, 1994, p. 183.

❖

Nothing seems more obvious . . . indeed anything but self-evident.

Immanuel Wallerstein, 'The Construction of Peoplehood: Racism, Nationalism, Ethnicity', *Race, Nation, Class — Ambiguous Identities* Balibar & Wallerstein, New York, Verso, p. 71.

❖ ❖

### 9.3   The kaleidoscopic self

*Question #1: Glasgow or Moscow?*

Ross Birrell material supplied by the artist and witnessed by the author.

❖

*Question #2: Woman or dress?*

Julie Laffin material witnessed by the author.

❖

*Question #3: Man or money?*

Text derived from William Pope. L news release, February 1, 1997, property of the author.

❖ ❖

### 9.4   Waiting for the Barbarians

Constantine Cavafy, 'Waiting for the Barbarians', trans. Edmund Keeley
*Against Forgetting*, ed. Carolyn Forche, New York, W. W. Norton & Company, 1993,
pp. 490–1.

*The Cambridge Biographical Dictionary*, D. Crystal ed., Cambridge, Cambridge
University Press, 1996.

❖ ❖

### 9.5   What is the world?

*Question #2: Is the world mistaken?*

The other in all his or her forms gives me I. It is on the occasion of the other that
I catch sight of *me*; or that I catch *me* at: reacting, choosing, refusing, accepting. It
is the other who makes my portrait. Always. And luckily. The other of all sorts, is
also of all diverse richness.

Helene Cixous and Mireille Calle-Gruber, *Rootprints – Memory and Life Writings*, trans.
Eric Prenowitz, New York, Routledge, 1997, p. 13.

❖

A hierarchizing spirit rages between individuals, between people, between parties.
All the time. The world is mistaken. It imagines that the other takes something from
us whereas the other only brings to us, all the time.

Helene Cixous and Mireille Calle-Gruber, *Rootprints — Memory and Life Writings*, trans. Eric Prenowitz, New York, Routledge, 1997, p. 13.

❖

There is a shock that happens daily, that is up to us to manage. There is a *positive incomprehension*: the fact that the other is so very much other. Is so very much not-me. The fact that we can say to each other all the time: here, I am not like you.

Helene Cixous and Mireille Calle-Gruber, *Rootprints — Memory and Life Writings*, trans. Eric Prenowitz, New York, Routledge, 1997, p. 16.

❖

*Question #3: What is rice?*

*Two Zen Classics* — Mumonkan and Hekiganroku, Case #5 of Hekiganroku, Katsuki Sekida, trans. A.V. Grimstone, ed., New York, Weatherhill, 1976.

*The Shambhala Dictionary of Buddhism and Zen*, trans. Michael H. Kohn, Fischer-Schreiber, Ehrhard, Diener, ed., Boston, Shambhala, 1991.

❖ ❖ ❖

# 10. THREE NOTEWORTHY DEPARTURES

❖ ❖

## 10.1 Nancarrow x 3

September 25, 1997, Goat Island Summer School Newsletter #1.

### 2: Exactitude (from Calvino)

> I began by speaking of exactitude, not of the infinite and the cosmos. I wanted to tell you of my fondness for geometrical forms, for symmetries, for numerical series, for all that is combinatory, for numerical proportions; I wanted to explain the things I had written in terms of my fidelity to the idea of limits, of measure . . . But perhaps it is precisely this idea of forms that evokes the idea of the endless . . .

Italo Calvino, 'Exactitude', *Six Memos for the Next Millennium*, Cambridge MA, Harvard, 1988, p. 68.

❖

*3: Ghost of 19 seconds*

David Murray, 'Minimalism and more', *Financial Times*, November 3–4, 1990.

See also:

Kyle Gann, *The Music of Conlon Nancarrow*, Cambridge, Cambridge University Press, 1995.

Conlon Nancarrow, *Studies for Player Piano Vol. III & IV*, Mainz, Wergo 60166–50, 60167–50, 1990.

❖ ❖

## 10.2   In Memoriam to Kathy Acker
December 18, 1997, Memorial Celebration of the Life and Work of Kathy Acker, School of the Art Institute of Chicago.

*2: Writing life writing death*
"I know I will love death when it comes, for I have loved life."

Rabindranath Tagore, '95', *Gitanjali [Song Offerings]*, Boston, Branden, 1992.

❖

*3: Everything is true*
Airplane understood, as everyone grows to or grows up to understand, that she needed a job. For since she knew blood could drip down her legs, she knew she didn't want to live on the street where there was no medical care. The minute you know you have to have a boss, you feel fear. Vice versa. She didn't know yet she now feared. The job was easy, the boss said.

Kathy Acker, *In Memoriam to Identity*, New York, Grove, 1990, p. 126.

❖

People frequently ask me what my definition of writing is. This is it. It is work. That is my conclusion.

John Cage, 'The Future of Music', *Empty Words*, Middleton, CT, Wesleyan University Press, 1979, p. 186.

❖

Work all day, work all night, 'till there's nothin' left of life but work.

Kathy Acker & the Mekons, *Pussy, King of the Pirates*, Chicago, Quarterstick Records, QS36CD.

❖

I never thought I had imagination. I've never fantasized. I've used other texts, or I've used friends. I've used memories. But I've never created stories by making things up. There's nothing mysterious. When I'm writing, my mind is focused on the present. Everything is true.

> Kathy Acker, 'Devoured by Myths (interview)', *Hannibal Lecter, My Father*, New York, Semiotext(e), 1991, p. 8.

❖

All that she gives, all that she is given, and still injustice has the greater part.

> What I give, what I am given, and still injustice
> has the greater part

> Odysseas Elytis, 'Entrance', *The Little Mariner*, trans. Olga Broumas, Port Townsend WA, Copper Canyon Press, 1988, p. 9.

❖

No one will make me again, no one from this earth. No one will cover over my ashes. No one. Nothing I was, am, will be. I'm blooming, this nothing – no one's -rose. With my pistil or soul, with my stamen which fate destroyed, my center's red by means of the red word, I sang, over and over, this thorn.

> Kathy Acker, *In Memoriam to Identity*, New York, Grove, 1990, pp. 125–6.

❖ ❖

## 10.3  Not eulogizing Lawrence Steger
Empress Elisabeth (1837–98); Ludwig II of Bavaria (1864–86).

> David Crystal, ed., *The Cambridge Biographical Dictionary*, Cambridge, Cambridge University Press, 1996.

❖

Empress Elisabeth anecdotes and Pestsäule details derive from:

> Jonathan Bousfield and Rob Humphreys, *Austria – The Rough Guide*, London, Rough Guides, 1998, pp. 120, 76.

❖

You told your story only through the stories of King Ludwig II of Bavaria . . .

> Lawrence Steger, *The Swans*, unpublished script in possession of the author.

❖

We write in haphazard fashion, page after page, the memories that poison us, spontaneously, without plan or system, as intricate and crowded as an anthill. We, who feel closer to the dead than to the living, continue, concise and bloody at breakneck speed, that through the telling we might become neither martyrs nor debased nor saints, but people again like everyone else.

> The things I had seen and suffered were burning
> inside of me; I felt closer to the dead than the
> living . . . I was writing concise and bloody
> poems, telling the story at breakneck speed . . .
> by writing I found peace for a while and felt
> myself become a man again, a person like
> everyone else, neither a martyr nor debased nor
> a saint . . . writing in a haphazard fashion page
> after page of the memories which were
> poisoning me . . .

Primo Levi, *The Periodic Table*, trans. Raymond Rosenthal, New York, Schocken, 1984, pp. 151–2 (Chromium).

❖

But we do not know the names of sickness . . .

> The Physician says I have "Nervous
>     prostration."
> Possibly I have – I do not know the Names of
>     Sickness.

Susan Howe, *My Emily Dickinson*, Berkeley, North Atlantic, 1985, p. 134 (quoting Emily Dickinson).

❖

Dennis said it: a friend of mine dies one night, grows pale as dust in a shaft of moonlight. You long to reach him again, all your life.

Now he and King Ludwig walk the same clouds, and when we think back on our lives full of dead bodies and bright as heaven behind us . . .

> A friend dies one night,
> swallows too many pills
> on his way to a party
> and grows pale as dust
> in a shaft of moonlight.

You long to reach him
again, all your life.

. . . Now you and
he walk the same clouds
only when we've been
stoned and think back
on our lives, full of
dead bodies, and bright
now as heaven behind us.

Dennis Cooper, 'Drugs', *The Tenderness of the Wolves*, Trumansburg, NY, The Crossing Press, 1982, p. 35.

❖ ❖ ❖

## 11.   FAILURE

❖ ❖

11.1 Failure: an elegy, September 27, 1999, exhibition essay, Transmission Gallery, Glasgow.

❖ ❖

**20**   He fell off the back of the high platform . . . so he couldn't even tell how he was going to land.

> Once we were performing *Nayatt School* in Philadelphia and I fell off the back of the high platform. During the last section, the destruction of the records, my chair went over and I fell over backwards. And there was a wild moment when I was in midair. It was dark, black, so I couldn't even tell how I was going to land. And as I was flipping in the air I saw Spalding up on top of his record player. It looked like he was shitting on it. And that was a very vivid moment of knowing what we were doing and the nature of records and recording and memory. When I landed, I broke my arm, and Liz stood up and said, "Obviously the play is over now."

David Savran, *Breaking the Rules: The Wooster Group*, New York, Theatre Communications Group, 1986, p. 120, interview with Ron Vawter.

❖

Once as a little boy in Fontiveros he had fallen into a pond.

> . . . Our Lady appeared to Juan in a dream.
> Filling his cell with light, she commanded him
> to escape, promising her assistance. This dream
> drew out an early memory. Once as a little boy
> in Fontiveros he had fallen into a pond. As he
> struggled in the mud and water he had seen a
> well-dressed lady on the bank whom he had
> taken to be the Virgin. He had stretched out his
> arms to her, but with closed fists because his
> hands were too dirty to take hers. Then someone
> else pulled him out. He now felt assured that, in
> spite of his weakness, with her help he would be
> able to escape from prison.

The Poems of St John of the Cross, trans. Willis Barnstone, New York, New Directions, 1972, p.14 (introduction, quoting Gerald Brenan, Horizon, 1947).

❖ ❖

**19** Franz Kafka, 'The Bucket Rider', trans. W. and E. Muir, The Complete Stories and Parables, N. N. Glatzer, ed., New York, Schocken, 1976, p. 412.

❖ ❖

**18** Susan Howe, Pierce-Arrow, New York, New Directions, 1999, p. 107.

❖ ❖

**17** Henry M. Sayre, A World of Art, New Jersey, Prentice Hall, 1997, p. 223, description of 'The Last Supper' by Leonardo Da Vinci.

❖ ❖

**16** We design our cities, but who will design their decay? . . . Through a revolutionary process of erasure, we establish a conceptual Nevada.

> More important than the design of cities is the
> design of their decay. Only through a
> revolutionary process of erasure and the
> establishment of "liberty zones," conceptual
> Nevadas where all laws of architecture are
> suspended, will some of the inherent tortures of
> urban life – the friction between program and
> containment – be suspended.

Rem Koolhaas and Bruce Mau, 'Imagining Nothingness', S, M, L, XL, New York, Monacelli, 1995, p. 201.

❖

We desire the permanence of the most frivolous item, and we desire the performance of instability.

> The permanence of even the most frivolous item
> of architecture and the instability of the
> metropolis are incompatible. . . . In Manhattan
> this paradox is resolved in a brilliant way:
> through the development of a mutant
> architecture that combines the aura of
> monumentality with the performance of
> instability.

Rem Koolhaas and Bruce Mau, 'Elegy for the Vacant Lot', S, M, L, XL, New York, Monacelli, 1995, p. 937.

❖

But what if a mistake simply reverses an earlier mistake?

> But what if his mistake had simply erased an
> earlier mistake?

Italo Calvino, Mr Palomar, trans. William Weaver, New York, Harcourt Brace Jovanovich, 1985, p. 100.

❖ ❖

15 Henry Petroski, To Engineer Is Human, New York, Random House, 1992, pp. 7–8.

❖ ❖

14 Jack Smith, 'Notes for a Ford Foundation Application', Film Culture No. 76, p. 24.

See also P. Adams Sitney, 'Writing Jack Smith's Ford Foundation Application', Film Culture, No. 78, p. 12.

❖ ❖

**13**   The Globe Theatre burned down ... February 12, 1990.

Alan Read, *Theatre & Everyday Life: An Ethics of Performance*, London, Routledge, 1993, p. 229.

❖

The craft apparently crashed in the New Mexico desert on July 3, 1947.

Jenny Randles, *UFO Retrievals: The Recovery of Alien Spacecraft*, London, Blandford, 1995, p. 33.

❖ ❖

**12**   Geoff Smith and Nicola Walker Smith, *American Originals – Interviews with 25 Contemporary Composers*, London, Faber & Faber, 1994, p. 39, interview with Laurie Anderson.

❖ ❖

**11**   Jim Hogshire, *Grossed-Out Surgeon Vomits Inside Patient! – An Insider's Look at Supermarket Tabloids*, Venice CA, Feral House, 1997, pp. 65–6.

❖ ❖

**10**   Failure subcategories (incomplete list) by the author.

❖ ❖

**9**   Rudolph Grey, *Nightmare of Ecstasy, The Life and Art of Edward D. Wood, JR.*, Portland OR, Feral House, 1994, p. 110.

❖ ❖

**8**   Robert E. Buswell Jr., *Tracing Back the Radiance: Chinul's Korean Way of Zen*, Honolulu, Kuroda Institute/University of Hawaii, 1991, from 'Secrets on Cultivating the Mind' written by Chinul between 1203 and 1205.

❖ ❖

**7**   The Center for Land Use Interpretation, *Hinterland – A Voyage Into Exurban Southern California*, exhibition catalogue, Los Angeles Contemporary Exhibitions, 1997, entry 1.

❖ ❖

**6**    Quests end in failure. One answer undoes another. Trust absence.

> Quests end in failure, no victory and sham
> questor. One answer undoes another and fiction
> is real. Trust absence, allegory, mystery – the
> setting not the rising sun is Beauty.

Susan Howe, *My Emily Dickinson*, Berkeley, North Atlantic, 1985, p. 23.

❖

Only fragments are accurate.

Lyn Hejinian, *My Life*, Los Angeles, Sun & Moon, 1987, p. 54, line 28.

❖

Once as a little girl she couldn't get the word butterfly so tried to get the word moth.

Lyn Hejinian, *My Life*, Los Angeles, Sun & Moon, 1987, p. 19, line 32.

❖ ❖

**5**    See 14 above, Jack Smith p. 25.

❖ ❖

**4**    Paul Virilio, *Politics of the Very Worst*, New York, Semiotext(e), 1999, pp. 12–13.

❖ ❖

**3**    A microstory by the author.

❖ ❖

**2**    James Gleick, *Chaos: Making A New Science*, New York, Penguin, 1987, pp. 91–2.

Benoit Mandelbrot, *The Fractal Geometry of Nature*, New York, W. H. Freeman and Co., 1983, p. 78.

❖ ❖

**1**    *The Life of Saint Teresa of Avila by Herself*, trans. J. M. Cohen, New York, Penguin, 1957, pp. 39–40.

❖ ❖

**0**    See 1 above, p. 40.

❖ ❖

## 00. TO THE READER-2

By now you must be tired of reading and ready to turn off your light. But wait.

> . . . "Turn off your light, too. Aren't you tired of
> reading?"
>> And you say, "Just a moment, I've
> almost finished . . . "

Italo Calvino, If on a winter's night a traveler, trans. William Weaver, New York, Harcourt Brace Jovanovich, 1981, p. 260.

❖

. . . to postpone a bit longer the moment of leaving.

> . . . they kept postponing till the next interval the
> moment of leaving.

Nathalie Sarraute, Tropisms, trans. Maria Jolas, New York, George Braziller, 1963, p. 2.

❖

Some books, full of opinions, resemble umbrellas.

> This is all that we ask for in order to *make an*
> *opinion* for ourselves, like a sort of "umbrella,"
> which protects us from chaos.

Gilles Deleuze and Felix Guattari, What is Philosophy?, trans. H. Tomlinson and G. Burchell, New York, Columbia University, 1994, p. 202.

❖

Why not end with poetry?

> I have rearranged and altered various lines from verses 92, 93, 95, 97, 101, 103, Rabindranath Tagore, Gitanjali [Song Offerings], Boston, Branden, 1992, pp. 56–60.

❖

They composed my paths.

> The art of "turning" phrases finds an equivalent
> in an art of composing a path.

Michel de Certeau, 'Walking in the City', The Practice of Everyday Life, trans. Steven Rendall, Los Angeles, University of California, 1988, p. 100.

❖

What I have put into words is no longer my possession . . .

> What I put into words is no longer my
> possession. Possibility has opened. The future
> will forget, erase, or recollect . . .

Susan Howe, *My Emily Dickinson*, Berkeley, North Atlantic, 1985, p. 13.

❖

I would rather simply thank you for paying attention. Because of you . . .

> Thich Nhat, Hanh, *The Heart of Understanding* – *Commentaries on the Prajnaparamita Heart Sutra*, Berkeley, Parallax, 1988, p. 54.

❖

. . . which you have almost finished.

> See Calvino note above.

# BIBLIOGRAPHY

Acker, Kathy, *In Memoriam to Identity*, New York, Grove, 1990.

—— *Hannibal Lecter, My Father*, New York, Semiotext(e), 1991.

—— & the Mekons, *Pussy, King of the Pirates*, Chicago, Quarterstick Records, QS36CD.

—— *Bodies of Work*, London, Serpent's Tail, 1997.

Adams, John, *Violin Concerto*, Nonesuch Records 79360–2, 1996.

Akerman, Chantal, *Directed by Chantal Akerman*, 1997.

Anderson, Sherwood, *Winesburg, Ohio*, New York, Random House, 1947.

Apple, Jacki, 'The Life and Times of Lin Hixson: The LA Years', *The Drama Review*, Vol. 35, No. 4 (T132), Winter 1991.

Associated Press, 'Japan's latest advance: Robo-roach', January 10, 1997.

Babel, Issac, *Collected Stories*, trans. David McDuff, New York, Penguin, 1994.

Balibar, Etienne, and Wallerstein, Immanuel, *Race, Nation, Class – Ambiguous Identities*, New York, Verso, 1988.

Barthes, Roland, *Writing Degree Zero and Elements of Semiology*, trans. A. Lavers and C. Smith, London, Jonathan Cape, 1967.

Bartók, Béla, *Concerto for Orchestra*, written for the Koussevitzky Music Foundation in memory of Mrs Natalie Koussevitzky, first performance, Boston, 1 December 1944, Boston Symphony Orchestra, Serge Koussevitzky conducting, 1943.

—— *Concerto for Orchestra*, Israel Philharmonic Orchestra, Zubin Mehta conducting, London and New York, Decca Records, 1976.

Beck, *Odelay*, CD-24823, Los Angeles, Geffen, 1996.

Becker,Carol, *Zones of Contention*, Albany, SUNY, 1996.

Beckett, Samuel, *Molloy, Malone Dies, The Unnamable*, London, Calder, 1959.

Betsko, Kathleen and Koenig, Rachel, *Interviews with Contemporary Women Playwrights*, New York, Beech Tree Books/Quill Edition, 1987.

The Holy Bible, Revised Standard Version, New York, Thomas Nelson & Sons, 1953.

Birringer, Johannes, *Theatre, Theory, Postmodernism*, Bloomington and Indianapolis, Indiana University Press, 1991.

Blum, William, 'U.S. Serial Bombing: The Grim Record', *CovertAction Quarterly*, No. 67, Spring–Summer 1999.

Borges, Jorge Luis, *The Aleph and Other Stories 1933–1969*, trans. Norman Thomas Di Giovanni and the author, New York, E. P. Dutton, 1978.

—— with Margarita Guerrero, *The Book of Imaginary Beings*, trans. N. T. di Giovanni, New York, E. P. Dutton, 1978.

Bottoms, Stephen J., 'Re-staging Roy: Citizen Cohn and the Search for Xanadu', *Theatre Journal*, Vol. 48, No. 2, May 1996.

—— 'The Tangled Flora of Goat Island: Rhizome, Repetition, Reality', *Theatre Journal*, Vol. 50, No. 4, December 1998.

Bousfield, Jonathan, and Humphreys, Rob, *Austria – The Rough Guide*, London, Rough Guides, 1998.

Boyer, Paul, *By the Bomb's Early Light: American Thought and Culture at the Dawn of the Atomic Age*, New York, Pantheon, 1985.

Brunelle, Ray, 'The Art of Sound Effects, Part 2', *Experimental Musical Instruments*, Vol. 12 No. 2, December, 1996.

Bryars, Gavin, *The Sinking of the Titanic*, New York, CD-446-061-2, Point Music, 1994.

—— '"Titanic" Final Hymn Given New Chords', *All Things Considered*, National Public Radio, April 14, 1995.

Buber, Martin, *Tales of the Hasidim – The Early Masters*, New York, Schocken, 1947.

—— *Tales of the Hasidim – Later Masters*, New York, Schocken, 1948.

Buswell, Robert E., Jr., *Tracing Back the Radiance: Chinul's Korean Way of Zen*, Honolulu, Kuroda Institute/University of Hawaii, 1991.

Cage, John, *Silence*, Hanover, NH, Wesleyan University Press, 1961.

—— *Empty Words*, Middleton, CT, Wesleyan University Press, 1979.

—— 'On Having Received the Carl Sczuka Prize for Roaratorio', *Roaratorio*, 28/29, Kew Gardens NY, Mode Records CD, 1992.

—— *Freeman Etudes, Books One and Two*, New York, CD 32, Mode, 1993.

Calvino, Italo, *If on a winter's night a traveler*, trans. William Weaver, New York, Harcourt Brace Jovanovich, 1981.

—— *Mr Palomar*, trans. by William Weaver, New York, Harcourt Brace Jovanovich, 1985.

—— *Six Memos for the Next Millennium*, Cambridge MA, Harvard, 1988.

Camus, Albert, *The Plague*, trans. S. Gilbert, New York, Vintage, 1991.

—— *The Myth of Sisyphus and other essays*, trans. Justin O'Brien, New York, Vintage, 1955.

Caruth, Cathy, *Unclaimed Experience: Trauma, Narrative & History*, The Johns Hopkins University Press, 1996.

Cavafy, Constantine, *The Complete Poems of Cavafy*, ed. and trans. Rae Dalven, New York, Harcourt Brace Jovanovich, 1976.

The Center for Land Use Interpretation, *Hinterland – A Voyage Into Exurban Southern California*, exhibition catalogue, Los Angeles Contemporary Exhibitions, 1997.

de Certeau, Michel, *The Practice of Everyday Life*, trans. Steven Rendall, Los Angeles, University of California, 1988.

Child, Mark, *Discovering Church Architecture – A Glossary of Terms*, Princes Risborough, Shire Publications, 1976.

Christian Farms, *Mike Walker Testimony*, unpublished recording in possession of the author.

Cixous, Hélène, and Calle-Gruber, Mireille, *Rootprints – Memory and Life Writings*, trans. Eric Prenowitz, New York, Routledge, 1997.

Cole, Susan Letzler, *Directors in Rehearsal*, New York, Routledge, 1992.

Cooper, Dennis, *The Tenderness of the Wolves*, Trumansburg, NY, The Crossing Press, 1982.

Croyden, Margaret, *Lunatics, Lovers and Poets – The Contemporary Experimental Theatre*, New York, Dell, 1974.

Crystal, D., ed., *The Cambridge Biographical Dictionary*, Cambridge, Cambridge University Press, 1996.

David-Neel, Alexandra, *Initiations and Initiates in Tibet*, New York, Dover, 1993.

Deleuze, Gilles, *The Fold – Leibniz and the Baroque*, trans. Tom Conley, Minneapolis, University of Minnesota, 1993.

Deleuze, Gilles and Guattari, Felix, *A Thousand Plateaus – Capitalism and Schizophrenia*, trans. Brian Massumi, Minneapolis, University of Minnesota Press, 1987.

—— *What is Philosophy?*, trans. H. Tomlinson and G. Burchell, New York, Columbia University, 1994.

DeLio, Thomas, *The Music of Morton Feldman*, New York, Excelsior Music Publishing Company, 1996.

*Dhammapada – The Sayings of the Buddha*, 'Yourself', trans. Thomas Byrom, Boston, Shambhala, 1993.

*The Dhammapada – The Path of Truth*, trans. The Venerable Balangoda Ananda Maitreya, Berkeley, Parallax, 1995.

Disney, Walt, *Our Friend the Atom* , Walt Disney Publications, New York, Simon & Schuster, 1956.

Dodd, Jimmie, 'Mickey Mouse March', Walt Disney Music Company, 1955.

Dostoyevsky, Fyodor, *Crime and Punishment*, trans. Constance Garnett, London, J. H. Dent & Sons, Ltd., 1977.

Duras, Marguerite, *Hiroshima mon Amour*, trans. Richard Seaver, New York, Grove, 1961.

—— *Summer Rain*, trans. Barbara Bray, London, Macmillan, 1992.

—— *Writing*, trans. M. Polizzotti, Cambridge, Lumen, 1998.

Dutta, Krishna, and Robinson, Andrew, *Rabindranath Tagore: The Myriad-Minded Man*, New York, St Martin's Press, 1996.

Dybek, Stuart, *The Coast of Chicago*, New York, Knopf, 1990.

Edson, Russell, *The Tunnel: Selected Poems*, Oberlin OH, Oberlin College Press, 1994.

Elytis, Odysseas, *The Little Mariner*, trans. Olga Broumas, Port Townsend WA, Copper Canyon Press, 1988.

Enzensberger, Hans Magnus, *Civil Wars*, New York, The New Press, 1993.

Etchells, Tim, *Certain Fragments: Contemporary Performance and Forced Entertainment*, London, Routledge, 1999.

Feldman, Morton, *For Christian Wolff*, hat ART 3–61201/2, 1992.

Finkel, Anita, 'Gunsmoke', *The New Dance Review*, Vol. IV, No. 2.

Forché, Carolyn, ed., *Against Forgetting: Twentieth Century Poetry of Witness*, New York, W. W. Norton & Company, 1993.

Foreman, Richard, *Unbalancing Acts – Foundations for a Theater*, New York, Pantheon, 1992.

Gann, Kyle, *The Music of Conlon Nancarrow*, Cambridge, Cambridge University Press, 1995.

García Márquez, Gabriel, *One Hundred Years of Solitude*, trans. Gregory Rabassa, New York, Avon, 1971.

Gleick, James, *Chaos: Making A New Science*, New York, Penguin, 1987.

Goat Island, *Hankbook – Process and Performance of It's Shifting, Hank*, Chicago, Goat Island, 1994.

—— 'Illusiontext', *Performance Research*, Vol. 1, No. 3, Autumn 1996.

—— 'Notes on How Dear to Me the Hour When Daylight Dies', publication in possession of the author, 1996.

—— and the Students of the Sunflower Community School, Chicago, 'The Incredible Shrinking Man Essay & Board Game', *The Drama Review*, Vol. 43, No. 1, (T161), Spring 1999.

Grafton, Anthony, *The Footnote: A Curious History*, Cambridge, Harvard University Press, 1997.

Grey, Rudolph, *Nightmare of Ecstasy, The Life and Art of Edward D. Wood, JR.*, Portland OR, Feral House, 1994.

Hanh, Thich Nhat, *The Heart of Understanding – Commentaries on the Prajnaparamita Heart Sutra*, Berkeley, Parallax, 1988.

—— *The Diamond that Cuts through Illusion – Commentaries on the Prajnaparamita Diamond Sutra*, Berkeley, Parallax, 1992.

—— *Thundering Silence – Sutra on the Better Way to Catch a Snake*, Berkeley, Parallax Press, 1993.

Hawkinson, Tim, 'Shatter', polyester and aluminum, 84" x 84", courtesy of ACE Gallery, New York, 1998.

Hejinian, Lyn, *My Life*, Los Angeles, Sun & Moon, 1987.

Herzog, Werner, *Every Man for Himself and God Against All – The Mystery of Kaspar Hauser*, film, 1974.

Heschel, Abraham Joshua, *I Asked for Wonder*, S. H. Dresner, ed., New York, Crossroad, 1996.

Hijikata, Tatsumi, 'Kazedaruma', trans. Nippon Services Corp., *Butoh – Dance of the Dark Soul*, New York, Aperture, 1985.

Hillman, James, *The Dream and the Underworld*, New York, Harper & Row, 1979.

Hixson, Lin, 'Soldier, Child, Tortured Man – The Making of a Performance', *Contact Quarterly*, Summer 1990.

—— 'Generating Movement for Our New Performance', unpublished document in possession of author, 1996.

Hogshire, Jim, *Grossed-Out Surgeon Vomits Inside Patient! – An Insider's Look at Supermarket Tabloids*, Venice CA, Feral House, 1997.

Howe, Susan, *My Emily Dickinson*, Berkeley, North Atlantic, 1985.

—— *Pierce-Arrow*, New York, New Directions, 1999, p. 107.

Ibuse, Masuji, *Black Rain*, trans. John Bester, New York, Kodansha, 1979.

Irving, Washington, *The Complete Tales of Washington Irving*, New York, Da Capo, 1998.

Jacobson, Bernard, *A Polish Renaissance*, (20th Century Composers Series), London, Phaidon, 1996.

Jameson, Fredric, 'Marxism and Dualism in Deleuze', *The South Atlantic Quarterly* 96:3, Duke University Press, Summer 1997.

*The Poems of St John of the Cross*, trans. Willis Barnstone, New York, New Directions, 1972.

Johnson, Charles, *Dreamer*, New York, Simon & Schuster, 1998.

Joseph, George Gheverghese, *The Crest of the Peacock – Non-European Roots of Mathematics*, London, Penguin, 1990.

Joyce, James, *Portrait of the Artist as a Young Man*, New York, Viking, 1969.

Kafka, Franz, *The Complete Stories and Parables*, N. N. Glatzer, ed., New York, Schocken, 1976.

Kanigel, R., *The Man Who Knew Infinity: A Life of the Genius Ramanujan*, New York, Charles Scribner's Sons, 1991.

Kantor, Tadeusz, *A Journey Through Other Spaces – Essays and Manifestos, 1944–1990*, trans. M. Kobialka, Berkeley/Los Angeles/London, University of California Press, 1993.

Klee, Paul, *The Open Book*, The Solomon R. Guggenheim Museum, New York, 1930.

Koolhaas, Rem, *Conversations with Students*, New York, Princeton, 1996.

Koolhaas, Rem and Mau, Bruce, *S, M, L, XL*, New York, Monacelli, 1995.

*Kurtág, Lutoslawski, Gubaidulina*, Arditti String Quartet edition 9 MO 789007, 1994.

Latour, Bruno, *Aramis, or The Love of Technology*, Cambridge, Harvard, 1996.

Langer, Lawrence, *The Holocaust and the Literary Imagination*, New Haven, Yale University Press, 1975.

Leach, Neal, ed., *Rethinking Architecture*, New York, Routledge, 1997.

Lechte, John, *Fifty Key Contemporary Thinkers, from structuralism to postmodernity*, London, Routledge, 1994.

LeCompte, Elizabeth, 'Brace Up!', *Felix*, Vol. I, No. 3.

Lesser, Wendy, 'Speech With the Weight of Literature', *The New York Times Book Review*, November 17, 1996.

Levi, Primo, *The Periodic Table*, trans. Raymond Rosenthal, New York, Schocken, 1984.

—— *Other People's Trades*, trans. Raymond Rosenthal, New York, Summit, 1989.

Lynch, Kevin, *The Image of the City*, Cambridge, MIT, 1960.

McDonald, Andrew (William Pierce), *The Turner Diaries*, New York, Barricade Books, Inc. 1996.

McKee, Francis, 'Deep Blue', manuscript essay loaned by the author.

MacMillan, James, *Music of James MacMillan*, Catalyst 09026 61916 2, 1993.

Mandelbrot, Benoit, *The Fractal Geometry of Nature*, New York, W. H. Freeman and Co., 1983.

Melville, Herman, *Moby-Dick*, New York, Penguin, 1972.

Merton, Thomas, *Raids on the Unspeakable*, New York, New Directions, 1966.

Meyrink, Gustav, *The Golem*, trans. E. F. Bleiler, New York, Dover, 1986.

Murray, David, 'Minimalism and more', *Financial Times*, November 3–4, 1990.

Myles, Eileen, *School of Fish*, Santa Rosa, Black Sparrow, 1997.

Nagai, Takashi, *The Bells of Nagasaki*, trans. W. Johnston, New York, Kodansha, 1994.

Nancarrow, Conlon, *Studies for Player Piano Vol. III & IV*, Mainz, Wergo 60166–50, 60167–50, 1990.

O'Conner, Flannery, 'Everything That Rises Must Converge', *Everything That Rises Must Converge*, New York, Farrar, Straus and Giroux, 1970.

Oe, Kenzaburo, *A Healing Family*, New York, Kodansha, 1995.

—— *A Quiet Life*, trans. K. Yanagishita & W. Wetherall, New York, Grove, 1996.

Ono, Yoko, *Instruction Paintings*, New York, Weatherhill, 1995.

*Oxford English Dictionary*, Oxford, Oxford University Press, 1971.

Petroski, Harry, *To Engineer Is Human*, New York, Random House, 1992.

Phelan, Peggy, *Mourning Sex – Performing Public Memories*, London, Routledge, 1997.

Pook, Jocelyn, *Deluge*, CDVE 933, London, Virgin, 1997.

Randles, Jenny, *UFO Retrievals: The Recovery of Alien Spacecraft*, London, Blandford, 1995.

Read, Alan, *Theatre & Everyday Life: An Ethics of Performance*, London, Routledge, 1993.

Rich, A., *American Pioneers: Ives to Cage and Beyond*, (20th Century Composers Series), London, Phaidon, 1995.

Roy, Arundhati, 'The End of Imagination', *The Nation*, September 28, 1998.

Sandford, Mariellen R., ed., *Happenings and Other Acts*, New York, Routledge, 1995.

Sarraute, Nathalie, *Tropisms*, trans. Maria Jolas, New York, George Braziller, 1963.

Savran, David, *Breaking the Rules: The Wooster Group*, New York, Theatre Communications Group, 1986.

Sayre, Henry M., *A World of Art*, New Jersey, Prentice Hall, 1997.

Schwartz, Stephen I., ed., *Atomic Audit – The Costs and Consequences of U.S. Nuclear Weapons since 1940*, Washington, DC, Brookings Institution Press, 1998.

Scott, Kirsty, 'The fatal attraction', *The Herald* (Scottish newspaper), August 6, 1997.

Dr Seuss, *One fish, two fish, red fish, blue fish* , New York, Beginner Books: Distributed by Random House, 1960.

*The Shambhala Dictionary of Buddhism and Zen*, trans. M. Kohn, Boston, Shambhala, 1991.

Siegel, Robert, 'Reformed Racist Spreads the Word About Tolerance', Floyd Cochran Interview, *All Things Considered*, National Public Radio, air date June 5, 1995.

Smith, Geoff, and Smith, Nicola Walker, *American Originals – Interviews with 25 Contemporary Composers*, Faber & Faber, London, 1994.

Snow, Edward, *Inside Bruegel: the play of images in children's games*, New York, North Point Press, 1997.

Steger, Lawrence, *The Swans*, unpublished script in possession of the author.

Steiner, George, *Language and Silence – Essays on Language, Literature, and the Inhuman*, New Haven, Yale University Press, 1998.

Stevens, Halsey, *The Life and Music of Bela Bartok*, Oxford, Oxford Univeristy Press, 1964.

Stoker, Bram, *Dracula*, New York, Bantam, 1981.

Steven Stucky, 'Comments: Witold Lutoslawski, Symphony No. 4', Chicago Symphony Orchestra Notebook, February 20–25, 1997.

Tagore, Rabindranath, *Gitanjali [Song Offerings]*, Boston, International Pocket Library – Brandon, 1992.

—— *The Home and the World*, trans. Surendranath Tagore, New York, Penguin, 1985.

—— *Selected Poems*, trans. William Radice, New York, Penguin, 1985.

Tanizaki, Jun'ichiro, *Childhood Years*, trans. P. McCarthy, New York, Kodansha, 1989.

*The Life of Saint Teresa of Avila by Herself*, trans. J. M. Cohen, New York, Penguin, 1957.

Thornton, Leslie, 'The Last Time I Saw Ron', video, 1994.

Tranströmer, Tomas, *Truth Barriers*, trans. Robert Bly, San Francisco, Sierra Club, 1980.

Treat, John Whittier, *Writing Ground Zero – Japanese Literature and the Atomic Bomb*, Chicago, University of Chicago Press, 1995.

Tsatsos, Irene, 'Talking with Goat Island: An Interview with Joan Dickinson, Karen Christopher, Matthew Goulish, Greg McCain and Tim McCain', *The Drama Review*, Vol. 35, No. 4 (T132), Winter 1991.

Turner, Victor, and Turner, Edith, *Image and Pilgrimage in Christian Culture*, New York, Columbia University, 1978.

*Two Zen Classics – Mumonkan and Hekiganroku*, trans. with commentaries by Katsuki Sekida, New York, Weatherhill, 1996.

Ugresic, Dubravka, *Have a Nice Day – From the Balkan War to the American Dream*, trans. Celia Hawkesworth, New York, Viking, 1995.

—— *The Culture of Lies*, trans. Celia Hawkesworth, University Park, PA, Pennsylvania State University Press, 1998.

Volans, Kevin, *Dancers on a Plane, 5th String Quartet*, Collins Classics, 14172, 1995.

Virilio, Paul, *The Aesthetics of Disappearance*, trans. P. Beitchman, New York, Semiotext(e), 1991.

—— *Politics of the Very Worst*, New York, Semiotext(e), 1999.

Weisskopf, Victor, F., 'Teaching Science', *The Privilege of Being a Physicist*, W. H. Freeman and Company, New York, 1988.

Whitehead, Alfred North, *Modes of Thought*, New York, Macmillan, 1938.

Wiener, Philip P., ed., *Dictionary of the History of Ideas*, New York, Charles Scribner's Sons, 1973.

Wilson, Anne, *an inquiry about hair*, http://www.anu.edu.au/ITA/CSA/textiles/hairinquiry/, 1996.

Woolf, Virginia, *The Waves*, New York, Harcourt Brace Jovanovich, 1978.

# INTRODUCTION TO THE INDEX

To index means to point, as with a finger, like those comical signs shaped like an oversized hand with one finger pointing: to the cafe. This signage, as Alfred North Whitehead points out (*Modes of Thought*, 37), relates to the history of literacy. "About five hundred years ago, only a small minority could read – at least among the European races. That is one great reason for the symbolism of religion, and for the pictorial signs of inns and shops." Many images remain as traces of these times, when people met at the emblem of the bear, while the word "bear" meant nothing to them. Recently, I have begun reading books at the index. I have most often been disappointed by the skeletal limitation to proper names and specialized terms. At least a preliterate picture of a bear seems expansive in its meanings. The word "bear," alphabetized between "bean" and "Berlin," restricts the word to a reductive, pragmatic code, only loosely related to the book's intersecting networks of thoughts, words, and images. What is an index? It seems, in potential, like an alternative table of contents, a starting point for the left-handed reader, an alphabetized diagram of patterns, systems, and echoes: root systems, geological strata, musical themes. Take for example Robert E. Buswell Jr's inspired index for *Tracing Back the Radiance*, his scholarly work on the twelfth-century Korean Buddhist philosopher Chinul. This index includes a comprehensive list of Chinul's similes, including the following entries: "dust mote containing many scriptures," "groping for one's head," "mistaking a fish-eye for a jewel," "mosquito biting an iron ox," "word which splits nails and cuts iron." Such an index accepts the significance not only of poetic language to the philosophy under scrutiny, but also of the reader's need to return to these passages easily. We must remain aware of the small ways our languages imprison us, and plan our escapes accordingly. After all, a teacher may need to catalogue all the questions, an intern at the Museum of Jurassic Technology may require a comprehensive list of "accident" references, a curious meteorologist or poet may want to collect all the sentences which contain the word "rain." With this index, I have tried to accommodate the needs of these particular readers.

Instead of page numbers, I have used the microlecture numerical system found on the table of contents. I have abbreviated the Source Notes section with "s", and the Introduction with "I". For example, 4.1 refers the reader to microlecture 4.1, I2.2s refers the reader to the source notes for the Introduction section 2.2, IS refers the reader to Introduction to the Source Notes, and II refers the reader to this Introduction to the Index.

# INDEX